The Archaeology of the Roman Rural Economy in the Central Balkan Provinces

Rural settlements and store buildings

Olivera Ilić

BAR International Series 2849

2017

Published in 2017 by
BAR Publishing, Oxford

BAR International Series 2849

The Archaeology of the Roman Rural Economy in the Central Balkan Provinces

ISBN 978 1 4073 1503 4

Printed in England

BAR
PUBLISHING

BAR titles are available from:

BAR Publishing
122 Banbury Rd, Oxford, OX2 7BP, UK
EMAIL info@barpublishing.com
PHONE +44 (0)1865 310431
FAX +44 (0)1865 316916
www.barpublishing.com

Acknowledgements

First, I would like to express my grateful thanks to Dr Miomir Korać, director of the Institute of Archaeology in Belgrade and the director of the antique project *Viminacium, Roman City and Military Camp* for his cooperation and encouragement.

My grateful thanks go to my supervisor, Dr Miroslav Vujović, a professor at the Department of Archaeology, Faculty of Philosophy in Belgrade, for his advice and suggestions in the course of the preparation of this manuscript for publishing.

Also, I wish here to thank the many colleagues who, by their writing or conversation, assisted me in the preparation of this book.

My deep respect and gratitude go to the late Professor Aleksandar Jovanović for his valuable advice and information. It is thanks to him that this book acquired its final form.

Contents

List of Illustrations

List of Maps

List of Tables

viii

Preface

The book *The Archaeology of the Roman Rural Economy in the Central Balkan Provinces* brings together the results of the partially adapted text of a doctoral thesis defended at the Department of Archaeology, Faculty of Philosophy in Belgrade, in 2012 and new results of the archaeological excavations in the territory of the Central Balkans.

The study of the economic changes that took place in the time of the Roman domination of conquered territories is gradually becoming a focus of scientific interest in modern archaeology. In the context of those investigations, Roman agriculture should be examined because, besides mining, it was a fundamental part of the Roman economy during the entire Roman rule in the territory of the Central Balkans. Therefore, in this book we have examined the analysis of the so far discovered remains of material culture and their chronological determination, which reflect the social and economic changes following the arrival of the Romans in the 1st century AD.

The studies were aimed at obtaining information regarding the establishment of a new type of rural settlements (*vici*), the distinct forms of agricultural estates of the *villae rusticae* type, the building of special structures for storing provisions as well as the building of elaborate road networks for the transportation of agricultural products, in particular to the military camps on the limes where numerous army units were stationed. In the context of all this data it is possible to grasp the level of social development over the entire territory of the Central Balkans as an integral part of the Empire, and how this had an impact on all aspects of material culture. Using the results of field surveys and partial archaeological excavations, we have synthesised the archaeological material which, at this level of investigation, cannot provide a complete answer to the complexity of the problem. In that regard, this book should be understood as yet another way of comprehending the existing archaeological material, i.e., as a new contribution to obtaining more knowledge and a better understanding of Roman economic development and agricultural activity as a cornerstone of the development in the Central Balkan Provinces.

Abbreviations

Acta Arch. Hung.	*Acta Archaeologica Acacemiae Scientiarum Hungaricae,* Budapest
AP	*Arheološki pregled,* Beograd
APN	*Arheologija i prirodne nauke,* Beograd
Arch. Iug.	*Archaeologia Iugoslavica,* Beograd
AV	*Arheološki vestnik,* Ljubljana
CIL	*Th. Mommsen, et al. (eds.), Corpus Inscriptionum Latinarum* (Berlin, *1863–)*
Cod. Theod.	*Codex Theodosianus*
Digest.	*Corpus iuris civilis* vol. I, *Institutiones, Digesta*
Glas SKA	*Glas Srpske Kraljevske Akademije,* Beograd
Glasnik DKS	*Glasnik Društva konvezrvatora Srbije,* Beograd
Glasnik SAD	*Glasnik Srpskog arheološkog društva,* Beograd
Glasnik ZMS	*Glasnik Zemaljskog muzeja,* Sarajevo
GGB	*Godišnjak grada Beograda,* Beograd
ILS	*H. Dessau (ed.), Inscriptiones Latinae selectae I-III,* Berlin *1892-1916.*
IMS	*Inscriptions de la Mésie Supérieure I, II, III/2, IV,* Beograd *1976-1995.*
JRA	*Journal of Roman Arcaeology,* Portsmouth, USA
JRS	*The Journal of Roman Studies,* London
Lib. Or.	*Libanius, Selected Orations*
RVM	*Rad vojvođanskih muzeja,* Novi Sad
RMV	*Rad muzeja Vojvodine,* Novi Sad
Spomenik SAN	*Spomenik Srpske Akademije nauka,* Beograd
Spomenik SKA	*Spomenik Srpske Kraljevske Akademije,* Beograd
VHAD	*Vjesnik Hrvatskog arheološkog društva,* Zagreb
VVM	*Vesnik Vojnog muzeja,* Beograd
Zbornik FF	*Zbornik Filozofskog fakulteta u Beogradu,* Beograd
Zbornik NM	*Zbornik Narodnog muzeja,* Beograd
ZRVI	*Zbornik radova Vizantološkog instituta,* Beograd
ZRNMČ	*Zbornik radova Narodnog muzeja u Čačku,* Čačak
ŽA	*Živa antika,* Skoplje

1

Introduction

The spatial framework of the research in this book is limited to the Roman provinces that were formed in the territory of modern Serbia: the southeastern part of the Roman province of *Pannonia Inferior*, the central part of *Moesia Superior* (Map 1). In Late Empire: *Pannonia Secunda, Moesia Prima, Dacia Ripensis* and *Dardania* (Map. 2). This area has, historically, been associated with the flow of the rivers Danube and Sava to central Europe and Italy, and on the other side of the eastern parts of the Balkan Peninsula to the Black Sea. The valleys of the Morava and Vardar were in constant contact with the Mediterranean area.

Map 1. Roman provinces of the Early Empire, (After: M. Mirković, 1981, 73)

Map 2. Roman provinces of the Late Empire. (After: M. Mirković, 1981, 93)

Central Balkan provinces in the process of Roman expansion to the east, with the Roman legions at the border on the Danube and auxiliary troops further inland, were represented as an important factor in ensuring stability and peace in the region. In addition to preserving political stability, the task of the army was the involvement of the central Balkan provinces in the economic life of the Empire through the building of a dense network of roads and the establishment of urban settlements, military fortifications and the mining region.

The indigenous population was gradually included in the economic and social life of the Roman provinces. This process of Romanisation, which had started in the 1st century AD, can be explained by different factors. These range from the specific geographical location and the importance of roads in the land, the rivers on which trade took place between the Eastern and Western part of the Empire to the system of military fortresses on the Danube which represented the main line of defence against barbarian attacks from the north that turned up over the centuries and made *Moesia Superior* a strategically important province of the Empire. Administrative and military reforms, undertaken by Diocletian and Constantine the Great, formed the Roman frontier troops *milites limitanei* which represented the territorial units of the standing army. Their main role was to control and protect the borders of the Empire.

The archaeological material that is considered in this work chronologically covers the period from the arrival of the Romans in the 1st century AD and the beginning of Romanisation in the area of the entire Balkan Peninsula, to the middle of the 5th century, when it was destroyed by the invasion of the Huns

(441-443). Roman Limes on the Middle and Lower Danube and most of the cities and fortresses deep in the interior of the peninsula were completely destroyed. This event can be described as the end of the late antiquity and late Roman period in this region, and it would take a century to re-establish ties with the new capital of the east and the Danube limes once their importance was revived during the time of Justinian I in the sixth century.

Geographical and other natural features of the Pannonian-Balkan region

The area of the province of Vojvodina and central parts of Serbia are integral parts of a larger geographic area that can be described as the middle and lower Danube and central Balkan region. In the past, this area has been associated with Italy and central Europe by the flow of the Danube and Sava rivers in the west and to the Black Sea in the east. This area was also in contact with the Mediterranean world via the valleys of the rivers Morava, Nišava and Vardar. This area has very diverse geographical features that have determined various forms of human activity in the past. There is no doubt that each of the natural components of this region such as the landforms, the pedological soil composition, mineral wealth, climate characteristics, the hydrography and the flora and fauna of the area played an important role in the overall economy.

Northern region

The main natural features of the northern region are the large lowland rivers of the Danube, Sava and Tisza. On the course of the Danube there are numerous river islands and shoals, sand banks and great bifurcations, especially on the side of Banat (Vujević 1939, 1-29; Marković 1979, 18-24). In addition to these river valleys, characteristic elements of relief are loess and sand. These rivers were of great importance to the settlers of the region from prehistoric times, throughout the Roman period and up to the present day.

The early process of settlement of the area was also assisted by the characteristics of steppe-continental climate with favourable rainfall distribution that allowed for intensive farming. The mountains of Fruška Gora and Vršac stand out in the area of Vojvodina as features that form natural borders. On their slopes, numerous archaeological finds were encountered, not only of the Roman era, but also of earlier periods of human history. Mount Fruška Gora served also as a natural frontier rampart along the Danube towards the Bačka plains and the more barren areas. The natural obstacles that Romans faced in the course of their military campaigns can be seen from a brief description of the Tisza and the Danube confluence provided by Ammianus Marcellinus: *"Through these countries the Tisza meanders its way and flows into the Danube. While on its own, it flows more freely and slowly, weeps over long and wide areas. Near the confluence it tapers into a gorge defending the inhabitants from Roman invasions by the riverbed of the Danube, and poses an obstacle against barbaric incursions. Here the soil is damp and soaked due to rising rivers; it is swamped and covered by willows, and therefore it is impassable, and therefore it is impassable, except for those who know the terrain well. In addition, near the confluence of the Tisza, there is a river island around which the more powerful of the two rivers flows separating it from the land."*(*Amm. Marc.* XIII, 4).

Central Balkan region

The area south of the rivers Sava and Danube can be described as the central Balkan region. If we consider the geomorphological point of view, it is an area dominated by mountains which are intersected by rivers. This area is rich in fertile valleys and parishes that are enclosed by the mountains and gorges.

The fertile valleys are mainly spread along the river beds. Any of the natural components of this area: the geomorphic characteristics of relief, the pedological composition of the soil, hydrological characteristics, ore and mineral wealth, climate characteristics or the flora and fauna, certainly had an impact on the types of economic activities, as well as the way of life. It is difficult to set out in this brief review all the differences that exist in certain parts of the Balkan Peninsula. They are caused, on the one hand, by natural conditions and, on the other, by the stages of development of certain regions and the impact of various factors of civilisation.

The central part of the Balkan Peninsula approximately corresponds to the territory of the former Roman province of Upper Moesia (*Moesia Superior*). The area in the Velika Morava river basin together with the micro regions of Belgrade, Braničevo and Stig and western Serbia are the so-called Peripannonian region. It is different from the region of eastern Serbia dominated by plateaus and valleys, over which rise so-called island mountains (Marković 1970, 258-262).

A brief review of soil and hydrological characteristics

The area of middle Danube and the central Balkans can be described as an area that is very convenient for humans, bearing in mind the natural conditions and all the benefits that they provide for the active involvement in various economic activities. Among the important natural resources of the Pannonian-Balkan region, it should be mentioned that the soil is suitable for a variety of agricultural activities, and that there is a wealth of water, ore and mineral resources, forests and a multiplicity of flora and fauna. It should be added that an extensive network of roads that generally follow the natural contours of the land make this area a well connected entity. This has contributed largely to the fact that the area of the Middle Danube basin and the central Balkans has been a focal area for the broader region, with a significant population inhabiting it since prehistoric times.

Regarding the soil, we can talk about many different aspects, such as the vastness and distribution of agricultural and livestock areas, soil quality, and other natural conditions which result in higher or lower utilisation of agricultural land. Bearing in mind the different types of soil in the Pannonian-Balkan area, we can say that this area was suitable for agriculture to a greater or lesser extent. This was primarily crop production, depending on the characteristics of the land and on the processing technology.

In the mountainous areas of the central Balkans, agriculture was of a great importance to the population. It should be said that agriculture in this colder and wetter climate, with poor soil composition, has less options than in Pannonia and the river Morava basin. Arable areas were located mainly in the major river valleys of the mountains. However, these mountainous areas, covered with mountain herbs and mountain ground fruits, were very suitable for the development of animal husbandry. Animal products (leather, wool, cheese) were used not only in the home, but were also the subject of trade.

The great natural water resources of the Pannonian-Balkan include: rivers, lakes, curative thermal mineral water and sources of drinking water. Rivers have always played an important role in the overall life of the people. Their resource of quality fish allowed the coastal population to engage in fishing. Special resources were provided by the Pannonian Plain, such as numerous ponds, marshes and canals, where fish laid eggs and reproduced. Also, the bed of the Danube in the Iron Gate gorge served the same purpose for river-sea fish (sturgeon). No less important for fishing were the mountain rivers in the central area of the Balkan Peninsula. The significant advantages of this space were, in fact, that many rivers were navigable along their entire course, or in part at the mouth. The network of navigable rivers is located mainly in the Pannonian Plain, the Danube, the Sava, the Tisza, and in central Balkans the

Morava and the lower courses of a number of their tributaries. Among the navigable rivers, the Danube had special significance during the Roman period, and extensive work was undertaken to facilitate its navigation. All these navigable rivers allowed for the supply of goods for agriculture, mining, construction and so on. The Danube, as a very important river that flowed to the Roman limes, was used for moving the military river flotilla which monitored and protected the frontier.

Besides numerous rivers, the central parts of the Balkan Peninsula are rich in small lakes. However, they are rarely used because of their isolated location, away from main roads and in low density population areas.

The richness of the thermo-mineral waters and drinking water sources are particularly characteristic of the Central Balkan area and are comparable with few other places in Europe. They are mostly on the tectonic faults along the edge of the Pannonian Basin and in the central region of the Peninsula. Many of these thermo-mineral springs were converted into spas, places where the water was specifically regulated for medical purposes. It is known that the Romans had their spa and rehabilitation centre, *Aquae Orcina,* in the location of the modern Vrnjacka Spa, from the 2nd to 4th century. Drinking water from many springs was brought out to the settlements by aqueducts.

Climate and its variations in the ancient period

On the basis of data on global climate variations, we know that, at the beginning of the 1st millennium AD, climatic conditions in some parts of Europe were not the same as today. The Climatic Optimum of the Roman period was reached in the 1st century AD. The average annual temperature in Europe was higher than today by 1-1.5°C. According to research, the Alps were green in that period and the boundary of the glacier was at least 300 m higher than today (Schlüchter, Jörin 2004, 46).

As the period for which there is available meteorological data is brief, historical information about migrating plant species should be considered. By tracking the history of vegetation, it can be established whether the climate changed and when. As evidence for this, data shows that, in the early Middle Ages, the inhabitants of Greenland were still engaged in animal husbandry and farming, and that cooling started sometime in the 13th century (Opra 1998, 166). However, this change in the average annual temperature of the Earth is not accompanied by uniform changes in all parts of the globe. Regarding global climate variations, the changes were greater in areas closer to the poles. Usually, major changes in the climate of regions with a higher latitude are followed by the moving of the borders of plants and the withdrawal of animals from these regions to areas with warmer climates, or vice versa.

Based on paleobotanical research, it can be concluded that the climate in the Mediterranean has been stable for the last few thousand years. Namely, the southern border of the grape growing region and olive growing region's northern border have not changed since biblical times. According to scientific knowledge, the northern border of the region of olive cultivation in Italy is in the same place today as it was during the ancient period (Opra 1998, 165). From data on global climate variations and its change around Greenland and stability in the Mediterranean, nothing can be concluded about climate variations in the area of the central Balkans. Grapes and chestnuts are characteristic of hot regions. Oak thrives in colder areas and can withstand very low temperatures, but bears little fruit. According to historical data, oak forests existed in the Balkans before the arrival of the Romans. The 5th century Byzantine historian Priscus, speaks of dense woods north of *Naissus* (Priskos, Frg. 8, 291, 23-26). The fruits of the forest are used for animal feed, but also for people. Bearing in mind the presence of these cultures today, we can conclude that the climate in the Balkans has not changed much in the last two thousand years.

Finally, we can conclude that the natural conditions of the territory of today's Serbia and central Balkan area were conducive to the development of agricultural production both in the Roman period and today. Lowland regions where agricultural activity could be performed on large, properly parcelled properties are characteristic only for the region of Pannonia and the valleys of the larger rivers, such as the area of *Viminacium*, the Velika Morava Valley and the area around the city of *Naissus*. Unfortunately, due to the lack of archaeological exploration, we still do not have a true picture of the importance and extent of agricultural activity in these areas during the Roman period.

It should be noted that, with all the positive aspects of the specified environmental conditions of the area, some negative consequences were sometimes exhibited which people, for centuries, overcame and that the struggle to master natural contradictions goes on today. For example, in some areas, relief was a factor of isolation and a barrier to linking different communities with all the consequences of economic, social, political and cultural life of populations. It was, therefore, necessary to build roads through such relief barriers in order to connect the different natural and socio-economic elements. Nevertheless, the natural environment of the Balkan region is, basically, very suitable for human life and for multiple and diverse economic, and other, activities. Besides the favourable geophysical benefits, the whole life of the population was affected by natural resources and by the new organisation of agricultural production that the Romans brought. The establishment of the Roman government in this area, as well as other socio-economic conditions, also had a profound effect on the population.

Such is its position in the Balkans, at the crossroads of major routes, that the area of modern Serbia early on began to receive cultural influences ranging from the prehistoric period, through the Greek and Roman eras and on to the Byzantine and Slavic periods of domination. Furthermore, this area has been provided with, in certain periods, the conditions for the development of its own culture, while on the other hand remained a peripheral area of cultural centres formed mainly in the Mediterranean. However, despite all these different cultural streams, and due to its great geopolitical importance, the area has been exposed along with all the consequences that arise from this very position, which is reflected in the offensives of various invaders and the frequent migrations.

The study of Roman rural economy and the previous work

Felix Kanitz, an associate of the Academy of Science in Vienna was one of the first investigators who, in his works, laid a foundation for studying the antique past in the territory of the Balkan Peninsula in the 19th century. An important place in his description of the Principality and, later, the Kingdom of Serbia was also devoted to the Roman heritage. He gathered the results of his investigations lasting many years into a large book entitled *Römische Studien in Serbien*, published in 1892. This book became indispensable for the investigation of the Danube Limes in the 19th and 20th century. His second major work, in two volumes, *Das Königreich Serbien und das Serbenvolk von der Römerzeit bis zur Gegenvart, Land un Bevölkerung I-II* was published in 1904 and in 1909, and is, even today, the foundation of archaeological investigations of many regions in Serbia. His use of earlier sources was not limited only to Roman itineraries but he also used numerous works from the 18th and 19th centuries, published as separate books or as studies in periodical publications. Among the works that Kanitz most often consulted was the major work *Danubius Pannonico-Mysicus observationibus geographicis*, *astronomicis, hydrographicis, historicis, physicis, perulustratus*, I-VI,[1] by L. F. Marsili, the Italian count serving at the Austrian court. Besides a study of flora and fauna and meteorological surveys, the book also included cultural heritage on the banks of the Danube. His works, in some cases, could be regarded as historical sources, as many structures are no longer visible in the way that they would have been in the 18th century.

The works of these two great explorers represented, and still represent, the basis for further investigations of the antique past in the Central Balkans region. Unfortunately, even to the present, investigations and the study of Roman rural settlements (*vici, pagi, villae rusticae*), structures for storing and supplying agricultural products and objects which served diverse purposes in Roman agriculture, have not significantly improved. Frequently, there only exist cases of incompletely recorded sites with no detailed description and this impedes their analysis and, in particular, their scientific interpretation. Only a small portion of the territory has been thoroughly surveyed (the region of Srem in Vojvodina and Mačva and the Drina valley in north-western Serbia). Significant results have been obtained by test trenching or systematic excavations, but there are only a few such sites. We could easily say that the study of Roman agriculture is, in the broadest sense, still one of the most neglected fields of classic archaeology in Serbia. While in the foreign literature interest in Roman agriculture within the general economic development has, in the recent decades, gained more and more in importance, along with the development of Roman provincial archaeology, this theme in Serbia is still isolated so that, even today, there is no genuine synthesis in this field of archaeology. The study of Roman villas has lasted over 200 years and numerous examples from the territory of the Empire, from the Black Sea to Portugal and from Yorkshire to The Sahara have been investigated in that period. J. T. Smith compiled a comprehensive typology of the villas using a survey of around 500 plans of those structures built throughout the Roman Empire. This has made possible the comparison of the similarities and differences in the construction of the various buildings (John Thomas Smith, *Roman Villas: A Study in Social Structure*, London 1997).

Between the two World Wars, two great men of Serbian archaeology, Miodrag Grbić and Nikola Vulić, studied the antique period in Serbia and Vojvodina. In the monograph *Vojvodina I*, published in Novi Sad in 1939, N. Vulić presents a description of all the then known archaeological sites from the Roman period, together with historical comments. Despite the fact that archaeological investigations had, in almost all these sites, not been conducted, Vulić still very clearly manages to define the character of the sites.

Immediately after the Second World War, the first significant topographic investigations were carried out by Milutin and Draga Garašanin who, in the monograph *Arheološka nalazišta u Srbiji*, published in 1951, presented all the known sites from prehistory and the Roman times in the territory of Serbia and Vojvodina. A period of large archaeological excavations, both of a rescue or systematic character, commenced in the 1950s and has continued to the present day.

In 1970, Miloje Vasić published the first synthesis on Roman villas in the territory of the former Yugoslavia, (Römische Villen von Typus der Villa rustica aus jugoslawischen Boden, *Arch. Iug.* XI). The publication presented all discovered Roman villas in that period, together with an effort to include their typological and chronological classification. Since that time, a considerable number of villas have been recorded in the territory of the Central Balkans. Nevertheless, works about villas were generally limited to a description of architectural remains or other objects, which were obtained most often by way of a site survey or they were chance finds and lacked the necessary data about the objects' provenance.

---

[1] Book was published in six volumes in Latin, in The Hague, in 1726.

If we look at archaeological investigations according to regions, we may notice that a somewhat greater level of investigation is recorded in the territory of the Vojvodina province. Thanks to the rescue archaeological excavations in recent decades, many scientific and scholarly papers have been published concerning the archaeological material from rural settlements, *vici, pagi* or *villae rusticae*. Besides the architectural remains of residential and economic structures, great attention was also paid to the study of archaeological finds. In that period, the greatest contribution to archaeology in the analysis of available material concerning various aspects of Roman agriculture in the south-eastern part of the Pannonia province has been provided by Olga Brukner and Velika Dautova-Ruševljan in their numerous scientific works published in periodical publications: *Rad vojvođanskih muzeja, Građa za proučavanje spmenika kulture Vojvodine or Arheološki pregled.*

Archaeologists from the Institute for the Protection of Cultural Monuments in Novi Sad and Sremska Mitrovica have, in the last four decades, recorded in detail, until then, unknown archaeological finds from the Roman period, including *villae rusticae* in Beočin and Šašinci. A more comprehensive picture of the archaeological sites in Srem was obtained in the course of rescue archaeological investigations along the route of the modern Beograd-Šid highway that were conducted in the period between 1973 and 1987 (*Arheološka istraživanja duž autoputa kroz Srem,* Novi Sad 1995). Although most of the sites were recorded only on the basis of the surface finds, we still may conclude that the archaeological map of Srem has changed to a great extent.

Results of the investigation of the material culture related to the Roman architecture in the central parts of Serbia, to the south of the rivers Sava and Danube, are somewhat less abundant. Site surveying of the terrain resulted in the recording of a considerable number of villas, but only few of them were explored by test trenching or systematic excavations. To date, the most thoroughly investigated regions are the areas of the Mačva and the Drina Valley where, in the 1950s, The Institute of Archaeology of SASA undertook a systematic survey, which was subsequently published as the monograph *Arheološki spomenici i nalazišta u Srbiji I, zapadna Srbija,* in 1953. However, the greatest contribution to the topography of that region resulted from the systematic survey that was undertaken by The Institute of Archaeology in Belgrade and The National Museum in Šabac, in the 1970s. Sometime later, small test trench excavations were also carried out. The results of those investigations were presented to the academic audience by Miloje Vasić, one of the investigators, in the journal *Glasnik SAD* 2, in 1985.

In the Drina Valley and in western Serbia, villas at Višesava near Bajina Bašta and in the vicinity of Čačak were separately explored. In central and eastern Serbia, villas in Poskurice near Kragujevac, in Gamzigrad near Zaječar, which was built before the imperial palace, and in Krivelj near Bor have been recorded.

We have more information concerning the villas in the territory of antique Niš in the book *Niš u antičko doba,* published in 1976, by P. Petrović. More recently, S. Stamenković presented a record of Roman villas in the Leskovac Valley in south-eastern Serbia, in the monograph *Rimsko nasleđe u Leskovačkoj kotlini,* published in Belgrade in 2013.

Concerning the immediate surroundings, it should be mentioned that *villae rusticae* are numerous in neighbouring Hungary. E. Thomas, the great expert in rural architecture of the Roman province of Pannonia studied the problem of Roman villas in her book *Römische Villen in Pannonien, Beiträge zur Pannonischen Siedlungsgeschichte,* published in Budapest in 1964. Despite being written more than half a century ago, this monograph is, even today, an indispensable source for the study of Roman villas within the wider territory of Central Europe. In the book, numerous examples of Roman villas in the Pannonia province (152 villas) are systematically examined according to geographic region. The typological and chronological classification presented in the study is, even today, extremely relevant in Roman archaeology. Recent investigations have revealed the wide distribution of villas in the territory of present-day Croatia, as in the Pannonia province. These investigations have been published by T. Leleković and A. Rendić-Miočević in *Rural Settlements, The Archaeology of Roman Southern Pannonia*, edited by B. Migotti, Oxford 2012, as well as in Dalmatia, by V. Begović and I. Schrunk, Maritime Villas on the Eastern Adriatic Coast (Roman Histria and Dalmatia), in *The Roman Empire and Beyond* (edited by E. De Sena and H. Dobrzanska), Oxford 2011.

The problems related to supplying and storing agricultural products intended primarily for the Roman army stationed along the Danube Limes in the Upper Moesia province has been thoroughly examined by P. Petrović, who analysed the topic in a few treatises published in scholarly journals. Besides the collection point at Porečka Reka, a few smaller military granaries have been recorded within fortifications on the Danube Limes and were mentioned in reports detailing the large rescue excavations at the limes, Djerdap I and Djerdap II, carried out between 1960s and 1980s.

Taking into account all the previously mentioned information from the short survey of investigations conducted so far, it can be concluded that the study of Roman rural settlements, villas and other economic structures related to agricultural activity, supply and transportation could allow a better comprehension of all aspects of Roman agronomy as a field of classical archaeology that is still developing, and should achieve a distinct physiognomy in the forthcoming period. Accordingly, this work should be recognised as a new contribution to the better comprehension and understanding of Roman economic development, with the agricultural activity an essential element of that development.

2

Rural Economy and Social Economic Development

Romanisation and urbanisation of the Central Balkans area and inclusion in the Roman economic system

Research on the economic activities in the Roman provinces of the Pannonian-Balkan area still has not provided sufficient information with which it would be possible to reconstruct the economic life during the Roman domination. In addition, the main difficulty is the lack of archaeological studies dealing with this topic. Taking into account its natural potential, it seems reasonable to presume that agriculture was the main activity of this region prior to its incorporation into the Roman Empire.

In pre-Roman times, the population of the Central Balkans lived mainly in rural areas. The changes that occurred following the Roman conquest have been traced largely from material remains, due to the lack of written sources. In the absence of urban agglomerations, the Romans relied on *civitates peregrinae* in the early stages. The process of romanisation and urbanisation was carried out intensively in the territory of Pannonia, unlike in other, more mountainous, areas in the south, which were difficult to approach. The study of the process of the urbanisation of the region north of the river Sava is based on sparse material remains. In the opinion of the investigator, there were *civitas Sirmiensium et Amantinorum* and *civitas Scordiscorum* in the territory of present-day Srem in Vojvodina, which would become the suburban area of the future city of *Sirmium* and *Bassiana*. *Civitas Sirmiensium et Amantinorum* was probably created at the end of the 1ˢᵗ century BC or the early 1ˢᵗ century AD (Mirković 2006, 29-35). Within the provincial administrative authorities, the *civitas peregirna* was under the military control of the prefect or local leader, the *princeps*.

The inclusion of the territory of Upper Moesia into the Roman administrative system took a little longer compared to Pannonia. The slow acceptance of change is especially noticeable in those areas that were remote from main roads or mines. Prior to the arrival of the Romans, the majority of the population lived in rural areas. Unfortunately, there is little information available regarding those settlements, such that the archaeological material only indicates the pre-Roman and early Roman period. Sources refer to aboriginal settlements, *oppida*, as the seat of tribal leaders and as a shelter in the event of an enemy attack. However, despite the more difficult circumstances in the territory of Upper Moesia, the Roman authorities sought the inclusion of the captured area into the Roman administrative system, which was implemented through the administrative unit – the *civitates peregrinae*. This has been confirmed by the inscription *civitates Moesiae et Triballiae* in the area of the River Timok (eastern Serbia), from the time of Claudius. In the inscription it is mentioned that the *civitates Moesiae et Triballiae* was under the direction of a centurion of the legion *V Macedonica, Baebio Attico* (*CIL* V 1838; *ILS* 1349).

Over time, the increasing involvement of the indigenous population in the Roman military service, the auxiliary units, led to the acquisition of privileges. The Romans did not show a tendency towards the faster urbanisation of Lower Pannonia and Upper Moesia so, until the time of the Flavian dynasty, there was no urban agglomeration in this territory. Urban centres began to develop along major trade routes, in the vicinity of mines or near military camps. The settling of the veterans around *Sirmium* or near military camps in the frontier zone of the Danube Limes began at the time of the Roman wars on the Danube. An inscription on a boundary stone discovered in the village of Beočin, near the Danube, provides evidence of the allocation of land to *Titus Claudius Priscilla*, prefect of the auxiliary detachment /*ala I c(ivium) R(omanorum)*/, in the territory of the village of Josista (*Vicus Iosista*), which dates back to the 1st century AD (Mirković 1971, 81-82, no 79, pl. XII/1).

The indigenous population mostly lived in rural areas in the wider urban territory, and had the status of free peasants. Based on the mostly epigraphic stored material, only an incomplete picture of the population and its socio-economic status of the time can be created. Namely, in the preserved epigraphic data, we find mainly the upper layers of the urban population which at first consisted of immigrant Romans and later, in the 2nd and 3rd century, they were joined by Romanised natives (Mirković 1981, 81-83). The socially lower category in cities and rural dwellers were rarely portrayed on monuments, so the knowledge that we have of this category of the population is insufficient for making more general conclusions about their origins and activities. As Romanisation mostly influenced the urban areas on the lower Sava River in Pannonia and the Danube Limes, it is assumed that most of the people from other less accessible areas had retained their language, rural way of life and economy by the end of antiquity.

When we talk about the different types of economic activities, the territory of the Central Balkans, throughout antiquity, stood out as an agricultural sector, remaining under-urbanised. According to recent studies of the economics of the Late Empire, this area was important as the land of the imperial domain of large landholdings (Mirković 1996, 57-58). Based on current data, in economic terms, there were several regions in the territory of the Central Balkans in the period of late antiquity: large estates were in the territory of the city *Sirmium* (Mirković, 1996, 58-61) and *Naissus* (Mirković 1996, 61-63) and their surrounding territories; agrarian, insufficiently urbanised areas were mostly in the province of *Dardania* and the Lim Valley, (the area of today's south-western Serbia), as well as the Timok Valley to the east (Mirković 1996, 63-71).

Based on original data, which shows the features of the late antique economy in the Central Balkans, M. Mirković opined that in the 4th century there was an increase of large landholdings. According to data obtained from historical sources, epigraphic and archaeological material, the imperial domain included the vast expanses of the valley of the Sava in the province of *Pannnonia Secunda*, as well as in the central area of *Dardania* and in the east the valley of the Timok River, where there were mining areas (Mirković 1996, 71-73). The existence of imperial property is indicated by the name of the imperial procurator on an inscription from *Viminacium*, dedicated to *Septimius Severus*, which was the seat of the imperial government domain (Mirković 1968, 138).

Due to their low economic and social status, the names of those who worked in public and private properties do not appear in descriptions, so one can scientifically debate only on the basis of assumptions. It is known that slaves certainly worked on the estates of soldiers and veterans. This is indicated by data from the 3rd century, in which is stated the allocation of land that soldiers assigned to slaves and cattle (Mirković 1968, 138). As well as slaves, peasant tenants also probably worked on these estates.

There is very little data available concerning agriculture. It can be assumed that the production of wheat was one of the main agricultural activities, as testified by the presence of tools that were used for cultivation (Popović 1988, 33-108). In addition, written sources can also provide direct or indirect answers to this question. According to literary sources, from the somewhat younger period, the population of *Singidunum*, during the Avar siege of 584, was busy working in the field because it was harvest time (Theoph. Sym. *Hist.* I 3-4, 46-47). The latest results of archaeobotanical analysis from several sites in Serbia, also indicate that wheat was the dominant crop in the fields (Medović 2008, 154-160; Medović 2010, 103-107).

The growing of vines in Pannonia and the Upper Moesia Limes is confirmed in sources from Probus, who is mentioned as the emperor who encouraged agriculture, the draining of swamps and wetlands and the irrigation of land where it was necessary (Mócsy 1974, 272). This emperor is also attributed with the planting of vines in Upper Moesia around today's town of Smederevo (*Aureus Mons*) and the Fruška Gora mountain in Vojvodina (*Alma Mons*). *Namque ut ille* (sc. Probus)...*eodem modo hic Galliam, Pannoniaisque et Moesorum colles vineis replevit* (Aur. Vict. *De caes.* 37). Eutropius also mentioned *Aureus Mons* as a place where the vines planted (Eutrop. IX, 17). Animal husbandry was an occupation of a large part of the population in the pre-Roman times and retained its importance in Roman times. This is understandable, bearing in mind the favourable natural conditions for the development of this branch of agriculture. Livestock products such as wool and leather were used largely for the production of articles for daily use and one of the better known food products was the Dardanian cheese *caseus dardanicus*. Late antique sources describe *Pannonia* as a rich and cheerful land (*Not. Dign. Or.* XXVIII, 26). *Moesia* and *Dacia* were mentioned as provinces that were capable of supporting themselves with agricultural products "*Moesiam et Daciam provincias sibi quidem sufficientes.*" (A. Mócsy 1974, 299). Furthermore, the valley of the Morava River is mentioned as a place where horses were bred. On a papyrus from the beginning of Trajan's government, in the daily orders of the cohorts, *I Hispanorum* mentions a detachment which was sent to *Margum* in order to obtain horses (Mirković 1981, 86).

The least known factor in the system of Roman agriculture is the labour force and the part the indigenous peoples played in it. There is interesting data from sources that says that the parents of the future emperor Maximian worked around *Sirmium* as day labourers (Mirković 1996, 58). Further interesting data can be seen in the inscription from the valley of the river Lim (present-day southwestern Serbia) regarding a certain *Vurus*, designated as a *villicus* (Vulić 1941-48, no 335).

Property relationships over land

The occupation of the Balkan regions in the first decades of the 1st century AD and the placing of them under Roman administration resulted in changes to property rights regarding land, whereby a conquered territory was placed under Roman jurisdiction. Especially important for the development of the agricultural economy was the *ager adsignatus*, which was land marked by border stones, divided into cadastre entities and then allotted for cultivation. According to A. Mócsy, the term *adsignatus* indicates a deduction, when property of veterans was, by assignation, taken from the peregrine *civitates* and became an ager *exceptus* within the municipal territory (Mócsy 1959, 90-91).

When veterans were discharged from the army they may have been given land *praemia militiae* in addition to money. Accordingly, there were two types of discharge: *missio nummaria* and *missio agraria*, both epigraphically confirmed in the territory of the Balkan provinces of the Roman Empire. The practice of acquiring land, *missio agraria,* is often explained by the fact that financial resources were often insufficient to cover the expenses of a discharge. S. Ferjančić, who considered this question in her study on the settling of veterans in the Balkan provinces agrees with the opinion of Neumann, who believes that allotting land as a form of *missio agraria* discharge had been practiced during the entire imperial period, and that such a practice had also been confirmed in the 4th century. In one decree of Constantine the Great from 320, veterans are mentioned as being given deserted land parcels (Ferjančić 2002, 12; Neumann, *RE Suppl.* IX 1606).

Missio agraria was related to the deductions from veterans and the establishment of military colonies that started in the Balkan provinces under Tiberius and lasted until the time of Hadrian (Ferjančić 2002, 21-102).[1] Besides the organised settling of veterans, which was characteristic of the 1st century AD and first decades of the 2nd century, there was also the individual settling of soldiers on the limes and in the interior of the Balkan provinces (Ferjančić 2002, 129-181). Where the territory of the Lower Pannonia and Upper Moesia provinces is concerned, discharged soldiers from legionary camps, smaller *castra* or beneficiary stations most often settled in the vicinity of the places where they served as active soldiers. In the territory of Central Balkan there are epigraphically confirmed veterans who, after completion of service, settled in the vicinity of the legionary camps of *Singidunum* and *Viminacium* at the beginning of the 2nd century (Ferjančić 2002, 154-165). From the 2nd century onward, veterans also settled in the forts on the Limes: Lederata, Pincum etc. According to the opinion of M. Mirković, in those fortifications were most probably stationed parts of the *VII Claudia* legion (Mirković, 1968, 120). Where smaller *castra* in the Roman province of Pannonia are concerned, there is the epigraphically confirmed allotting of land to discharged soldiers. This is confirmed on a border stone from Dumbovo, near Beočin, on the slopes of Fruška Gora, in the frontier zone of the limes with an inscription above mentioning *Vicus Iosista*.[2] A more detailed interpretation of the inscription is offered by M. Mirković, according to which the settlement had been established by the process of veteran deduction in the second half of the 1st century AD (Mirković 1971, 81-82).

In the region of the Upper Moesia Limes, as well as in the other provinces of the Empire, veterans were often the owners of large estates. The position of free peasants who rented the land is still not defined, and all our knowledge about that particular question is based only on assumptions. M. Mirković, in her study on the Roman towns along the Danube limes in Upper Moesia, has assumed that tenant-peasants probably worked on the land of the municipal aristocracy. However, over the course of time their numbers diminished, primarily because of their increased engagement in military service, thus increasing the use of slave labour. This is confirmed by epigraphic data from the 3[rd]century where it is recorded that, along with the allotment of land, soldiers were also given slaves and livestock (Mirković 1968, 138).

Dedications to agrarian deities indirectly suggest that some veterans were engaged in agriculture. It is confirmed by one such inscription dedicated to the cult of Liber and Libera on a votive *ara* from the wider territory of *Singidunum* (Mirković, Dušanić 1976, 52-53).

I(ovi) O(ptimo) M(aximo) et/ Terrae Matri/ Libero Pat(ri) et Libi/re (!) *sac(rum)/ T. Aur(elius) Atticus/ vet(eranus) leg(ionis) IIII Fl(aviae) ex/ sig(nifero) P. K. q(uin) q(uennalis) Sing(iduni)/ dec(urio) col(oniae) Sirmens(ium)/ v(otum) l(ibens) m(erito) p(osuit).*

In the Late Roman period, besides significant changes in the social relationships and social status of agricultural producers, changes also took place in the army's organisation. These changes had a particular impact on the ownership of land. Units of the standing (regular) frontier army, the *limitanei*, which were settled in the military camps, had been granted land used as pastures (*paludes*) from the 4th century onward (Jones 1973, 629). According to the law introduced by Valens in 365, the *limitanei* were given rations of food for nine months and for three months they had wages in cash, while after the law of Arcadius from 406, they were paid completely in cash (Jones 1973, 630). The question of the character of the Roman frontier troops, the *milites limitanei,* in the Late Roman period, still includes

---

[1]   Besides the establishment of veteran colonies, there were also deductions without establishing colonies.
[2]   The border stone discovered in Beočin in 1909 is housed in the Archaeological Museum in Zagreb.

series of enigmas. The term *limitanei* is mentioned for the first time in an official document in 363 (*Cod. Theod.* XII, I, 56), where it is stated that these were troops stationed in the frontier zones of the Empire (Isaak 1988, 146). According to B. Isaac, the *limitanei* should not be understood as a simple village militia composed of soldiers-peasants, as earlier theories still accepted by many scholars suggest, but they represented territorial units of the standing army under the command of a *dux limitus*, with their main duty being to control and protect the frontier regions of the Empire (Isaak 1988, 146). On the other hand, the earliest information regarding *limitanei* who owned and cultivated their estates dates from the first half of the 5th century. It was prohibited by law from 423 that anyone except the owner could till land within the territory of the fort, *castellum milites*, and a law from 443 prohibited giving frontier land (*agri limitanei*) to newcomers and it could only be cultivated by frontier soldiers (*milites limitanei*) who were exempt from paying taxes (Jones 1973, 653-654).

Taking into account the remains of civil settlements of a rural type with wooden houses that have been encountered next to military camps on the Iron Gates Limes, dating from the period between the end of 3rd century and the time of Valentinian I (Petrović, Vasić 1996, 22), as well as finds of agricultural tools in the Late Roman layers of fortification (Popović 1988, 33-108), and certain finds discovered within some Late Roman fortifications[3] (Gabričević 1986, 71-91), we can speak with some degree of certainty about the existence of civil settlements in the vicinity of Late Roman fortifications on the limes from the 4th and beginning of the 5th century (Vujović 2012, 38-39). Whether these were settlements of the families of the *limitanei* or rural civil settlements that were established in the vicinity of camps in order to supply the frontier garrisons it is not currently possible to give a reliable answer.

Despite this theme having only been partially investigated, it is still necessary to point to the problems concerning the structure and scope of property relationships, which cannot be solved on the basis of available authentic material and material remains that we have at our disposal. We still do not know who owned certain plots of land and who worked them. What was the relationship between *ager publicus* and territories of distinct legions (*territorium legionis*) is unclear, and this is also the case in other provinces of the Empire. However, it should be emphasised that the results of more recent investigations where authentic data, no matter how meagre, still make it possible to comprehend to a certain degree the increase of large estates in the 4th century, although the borders between imperial domains and urban territories are still imprecisely determined.

---

[3] This includes parts of jewelry: bracelets, earrings, decorative pins and spindle whorls originating from the Late Roman fortification at Rtkovo.

15

3

Roman Rural Settlements

Vici

In the newly-created provinces in the Central Balkans, besides autochthonous rural settlements, which continued to exist, an organised urbanisation of the conquered area also took place following the establishment of Roman administration. According to investigations conducted so far, this process developed more intensively in the Pannonia region than it was the case in the barely accessible mountainous and hilly areas of the Central Balkans. The new organisation of the Roman state resulted in the establishment of new types of rural settlements, *vici* and *pagi,* which were similar in their type of dwellings to the pre-Roman settlements of the autochthonous populations. It has been concluded, on the basis of the topographic data of registered sites, that Roman settlements were established in the vicinity of main roads and at locations that made possible the exploitation of natural raw materials along with the employment of a labour force from the neighbouring native settlements. Before the agricultural estates of the type *villa rustica* were established, such settlements, which to a great extent resulted from deductions from veterans, were important production units which played a part in supplying the urban centres.

To date, the most thoroughly investigated *vici* and *pagi* in the territory of present-day Serbia are those in province of Vojvodina, i. e. Srem, whose territory was, at the time of Roman conquest, inhabited by the Amantini, Breuci and Scordisci (Mirković 2006, 19-22) (Map 3). The topographic position of settlements between the Sava and the Danube in the Srem plains indicates favourable natural conditions, which guided the native population in its selection of locations for the settlements. These settlements mostly continued to exist under the new political, economic and cultural circumstances. The fertility of land suitable for farming and stock-breeding, as well as the proximity of forests and running water is also confirmed by, among other things, the faunal remains of domestic and wild animal species (Blažić 1995, 331-346).

Investigations carried out in the region in recent decades offer potential solutions to the problems of the beginning of Romanisation in the Balkan provinces. They have revealed that most autochthonous settlements with a Celtic material culture were not included in the new urbanisation plan carried out by the Romans in the 1st century AD. These settlements existed as late as the Flavian dynasty (Brukner 1995, 137). Subsequently, the established smaller estates and the land assigned to the veteran inhabitants of these settlements were included in the economic activities of the nearest agricultural estates, thus creating an economic entity with the estate. According to E. Thomas, villas were located in the favorable natural surroundings in the vicinity of the native settlements or on their ruins (Thomas 1964, 355). Investigations in the Srem region have revealed that early Roman settlements from the 1st and 2nd centuries AD were situated in areas where later building complexes of the *villa rustica* type were constructed, or in their immediate vicinity (Dumbovo near Beočin, Hrtkovici, Šašinci, Krnješevci etc.).

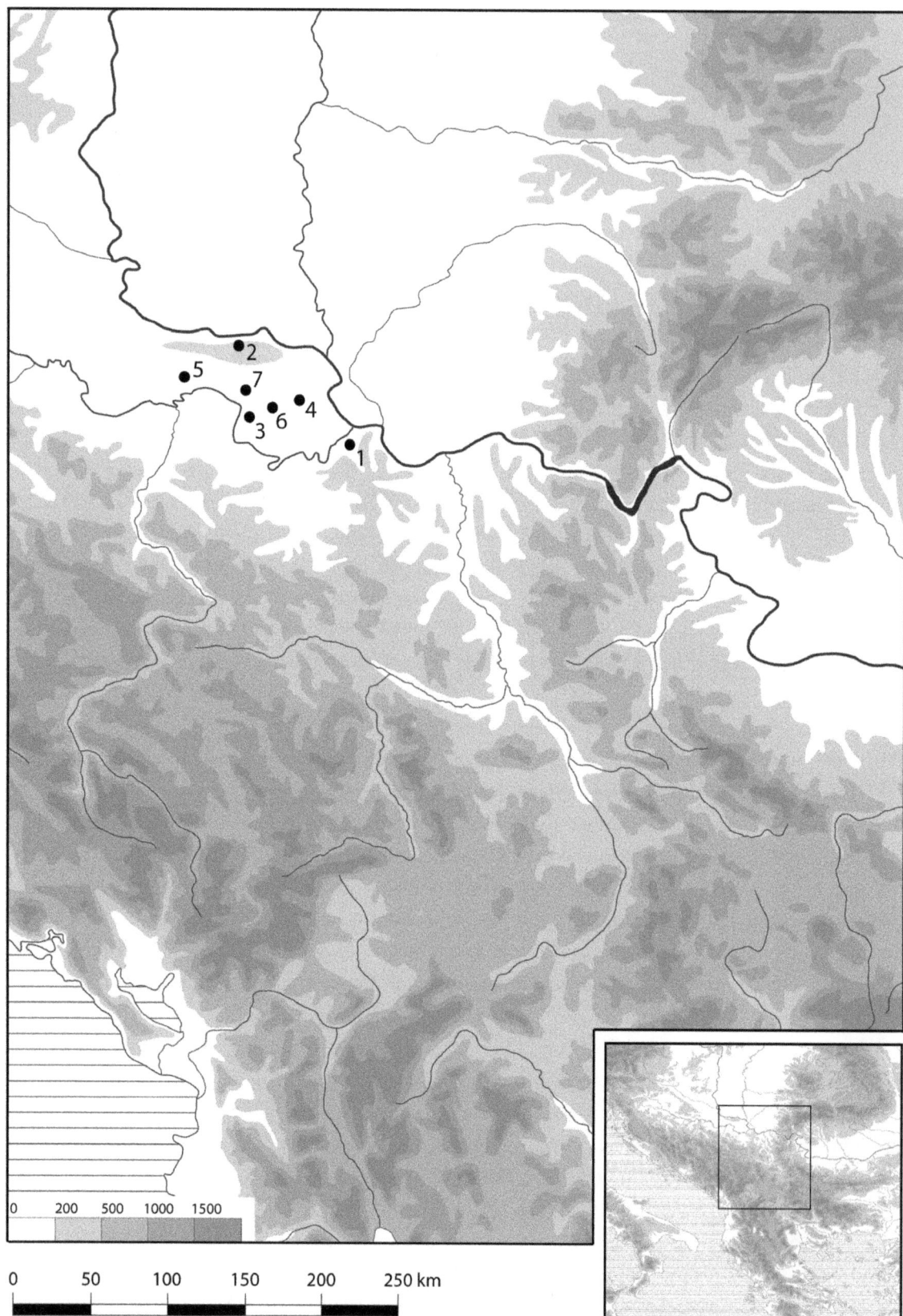

Map 3. Roman rural settlements (*vici*) in the territory of present-day Serbia: 1. Bube; 2. Dumbovo, Beočin; 3. Vranj, Hrtkovci; 4. Krnješevci; 5. Kuzmin; 6. Prhovo; 7. Kudoš, Šašinci

The main economic activity of the *vicus* inhabitants was, in most cases, agriculture, farming and cattle breeding. Besides this, depending on the availability of natural resources, forest exploitation and various kinds of handicrafts (pottery, leather and wool processing, crafts associated with wood-working, etc.) also contributed to the economic activity of the *vicus*. The processing of raw materials was, at first, limited only to satisfying the needs of the inhabitants and their immediate neighbours. However, later, via the trade routes, they reached more distant areas, thus becoming a segment of the economic life of the province.

The remains of *vici* and *pagi* in the territory of Upper Moesia remain mostly uninvestigated. For the time being we can speak with certainty only about one *vicus* – *Bube*, in the vicinity of *Singidunum* (Mirković 1988, 99-104). Its location in the immediate vicinity of the antique city confirms the assumption that *vici* were established near the larger urban centres in order to supply them with agricultural products.

Villae rusticae

The Roman villa is a term about which we could say to know a great deal, and understand very little. This claim was made by J. Percival in his book on Roman villas (Percival 1981, 1), and perhaps genuinely reflects our knowledge regarding this distinctive form of the Roman architecture. This is particularly true regarding the Balkan Peninsula, given that the level of investigation of villas in this area is relatively low in comparison to other parts of the Roman Empire. In addition, our view of these complex types of Roman residence still includes many questions, regarding the numerous typological classifications that express the distinctions between the various provinces of the Roman Empire. It is true to say that we actually know very little about the villas as social-economic units or about the lifestyle of their inhabitants. Our knowledge about villas is based partially on archaeological data, but also on preserved literary sources. They provide information about their organisation, their relationship with other forms of dwellings, about the structures that comprised an estate, and about the economic and social status of the owner, etc.

Marcus Vitruvius also wrote about Roman villas in his ten books on architecture, which represent the largest preserved work on antique building activity to date. In book VI, which concerns residential houses, a short passage is devoted to the planning and building of villas. In one chapter he offers advice on how to build a house on a country estate and what it should contain: *"Qui autem fructibus rusticis serviunt, in eorum vestibulis stabula, tabernae, in aedibus cryptae, horrea, apothecae ceteraque, quae ad fructus servandos magis quam ad elegantiae decorum possunt esse, ita sunt facienda"* (Vitruv. *De architect.* VI, 6, 5). Accordingly, for those engaged in farming activities, sheds should be built in the vestibules, and cellars, granaries and other rooms should be built in the house, as they are more suitable for storing food and crops than for beauty and elegance. He distinguished two categories of estates with villas – those intended for agricultural exploitation, called *villae rusticae*, and villas whose architecture emulates urban architecture and which are therefore called *villae urbanae*. As the primary subject of our work is structures and estates intended for agricultural activity, we will focus only on the *villae rusticae* as distinct types of agricultural estates.

It is stated in Tacitus that the word *villa* denotes all types of residences in the non-urban milieu (Tacit. *Hist.* V, 23; IV, 67; *Ann.* III, 46). Cato uses the terms *villa rustica* and *villa urbana* not to define character but to make a distinction between certain structures: in the centre of the estate are residential structures with urban comforts, *villam urbanam pro copia aedificat*, and then there are economic structures with mills, presses for oil, grapes and the like which he labels as *villam rusticam aedificatam habeat* (Cato,

Varro, *De agricult.* I 5, 2). In Digeste it is stated that: *"ager est locus qui sine villa est (Digest. L, 16, 27); fundus autem integrum aliquid est; et plerumque sine villa 'locus' accipimus (Digest. L, 16, 60); fundi appellatione omne aedificium et omnis ager continetur: sed in usu urbana aedificia 'aedes', 'rustica' villae dicuntur. Locus vero sine aedificio in urbe 'area', rure autem 'ager' appellatur; idemque ager cum aedificio 'fundus' dicitur (Digest. L, 16, 211)."* A *villa* is a building in the country, as opposed to one in the town, which is *aedes*. A *villa* and its land, *ager* form a *fundus*.

When speaking about the Balkan Peninsula it could be concluded, on the basis of investigations conducted so far, that by joining that territory to the Roman Empire in the 1st century AD, conditions were created for the economic and cultural integration of the autochthonic populations. New forms of production relationships and new cultural standards were gradually accepted which had an impact on the social differentiation of the native population. The development of new economic relationships as a consequence of assigning state lands to immigrants either within the agers of the colonies, within the territories of the *municipia* or on the estates of the veterans, resulted in the occurrence of a new type of agricultural estate in this area, the *villa rustica*. These were established outside urban centres and they had a primarily economic significance as centres of the rural economies in the given region. Despite being widely spread throughout the entire Empire, differences in their architectural concept or size were the result of climate conditions, geographic specifications, the purpose of the structures, the economic potential of the villa owner etc.

The urban concept of the villas depended on their character, whether they were imperial or landowner estates or smaller estates of free peasants, as well as on the economic activities practiced most by the people living in them. Roman villas could be classified according to diverse criteria, taking into account various elements. If we speak about the size and quality of construction and equipment, villas could be complexes of exceptional quality, luxurious residences, structures whose residential component was accompanied by an economic component, or the most numerous being those with a prevailing economic component with the residential and recreational character being of secondary importance.

The generally accepted division of villas according to the size of the property could also apply to the Central Balkans region where the following have been recorded: rather small village estates, 10-18 jugers with a residential structure and worked by the owners; estates of medium size, 80-500 jugers. On such estates the land and residential structure were generally managed by a *villicus*.

Archaeological investigations conducted so far indicate that mining and agricultural areas far from Italy, such as the Central Balkans area, did not attract Roman landowners until the 3rd century. Large estates appeared only from the time of the soldier emperors, although even then the imperial domains prevailed (Mirković, 1996, 57). An explanation for this is the fact that the beginning and middle of the 4th century was still a relatively peaceful period in this area. An unstable situation ensued only at the end of the 4th century when Gothic tribes started to increasingly disturb the relative prosperity of the Balkan provinces of the Empire with their plundering raids. The building of towers on the lateral sides of villas as well as specula near the structures speaks clearly of the progressively more turbulent times (Kudoš, Šašinci in Vojvodina). This trend was to continue into the first half of the 5th century, until 443, when the Hunnic invasion destroyed the majority of cities and rural settlements, many of which were never restored.

Villae rusticae in the provinces of Lower Pannonia and Upper Moesia, although recorded in relatively large numbers, have so far not been systematically investigated (Map 4). Currently, we are unable to distinguish with any certainty the number of identified villas and possible *villae rusticae*. We can

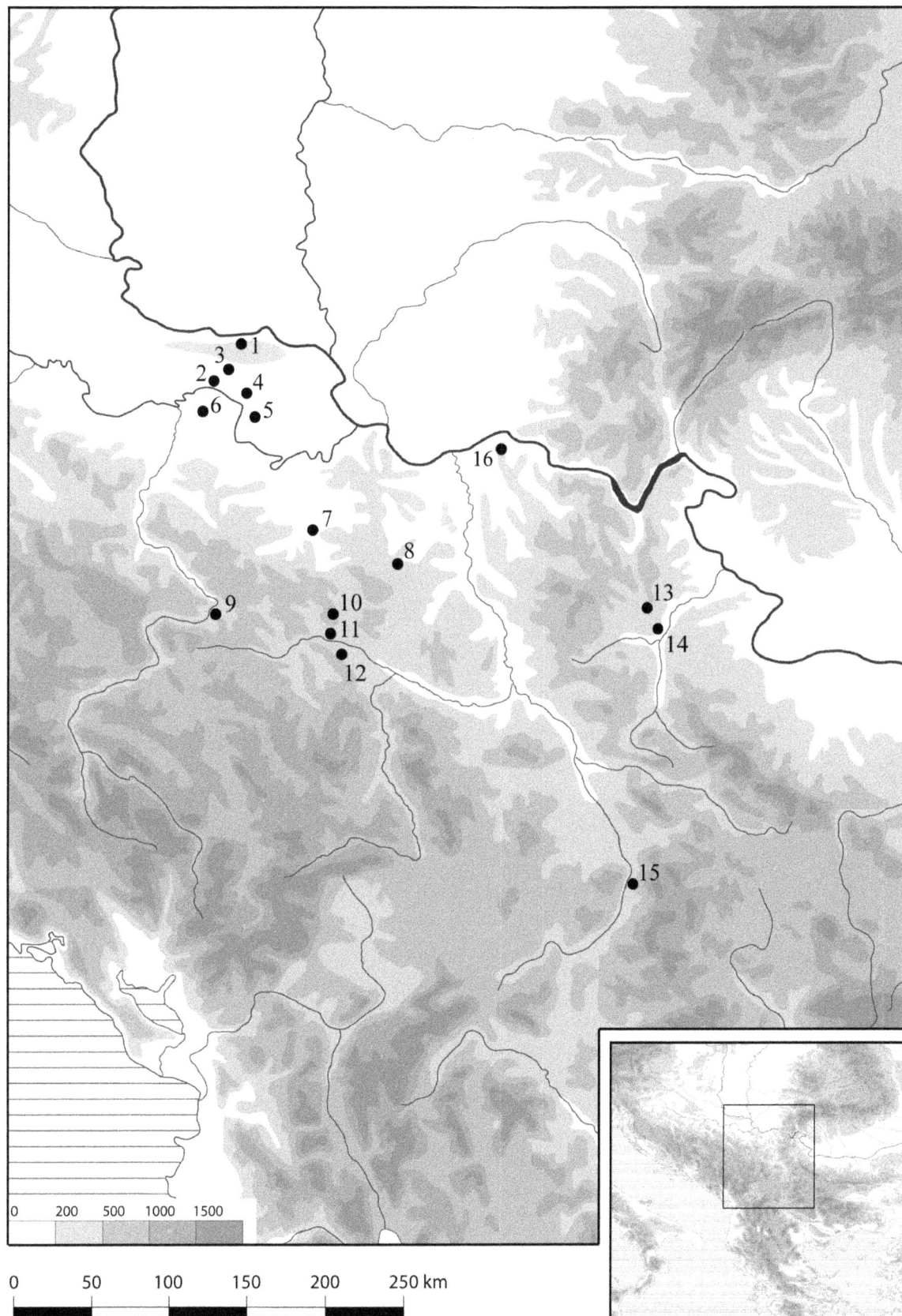

Map 4. Roman villas in the territory of present-day Serbia: 1. Dumbovo, Beočin; 2. Livade, Sremska Mitrovica; 3. Mitrovačke livade, Sremska Mitrovica; 4. Kudoš, Šašinci; 5. Vranj, Hrtkovci; 6. Štitar in Mačva; 7. Anine, Lajkovac; 8. Poskurice, Kragujevac; 9. Višesava, Bajina Bašta; 10. Gornja Gorevnica, Čačak; 11. Prijevor, Čačak; 12. Beljina, Čačak; 13. Krivelj, Bor; 14. Gamzigrad, Zaječar; 15. Kržince, Vladičin Han; 16. Viminacium

speak of the typology of those structures only on the basis of examples from the neighbouring regions, primarily Pannonia, thanks to great expert on the architecture of Roman villas E. Thomas, who made an overview of villas in the Roman Pannonia, including the territory of present-day Vojvodina (Thomas 1964; *Thomas* 1981, 275-321). One of the great difficulties when studying the problems of villas is the great heterogeneity of their forms and sizes. Some of the types, which are more or less recorded in the area of the Roman provinces of *Pannonia Inferior, Moesia Superior and Dalmatia* (Vasić, 1970, 45-81) include: villas with portico, Mediterranean villa type with portico, so-called villas with peristyle, villas with corridor, villas of a simple square ground plan and fortified villas with towers. Unfortunately, bearing in mind that most of villas in the Central Balkans are insufficiently investigated, a typological classification of those structures as well as their size could not be precisely established.

Region of Sirmium and Bassianae

A significant number of villas have so far been recorded or partially investigated in the course of site surveying and rescue excavations within the wider urban territory of the antique cities of *Sirmium* and *Bassiane*. A certain number of these buildings were built in the territory of the early Roman settlements from the 1st and 2nd centuries, or in their immediate vicinity (Šašinci, Hrtkovci, Krnješevci, Prhovo). The wider city territory of *Sirmium* has not been determined with any certainty, although its borders partially coincide with the earlier region of the Sirmienses and Amantini, *civitas Sirmiensium et Amantinorum*. The expansion of that area was limited in the west by the territory of the city of *Cibalae* and in the northwest by the territory of *Mursa*. It is still not known where the dividing line fell. In the north, the Danube formed a natural border along the line between present-day Sotin (*Cornacum*) and Banoštor (*Bononia*). The city territory of *Sirmium* bordered, in the northeast, the agger of *Bassianae* (Donji Petrovci near Ruma), which coincided with the territory of the Scordisci tribe, *civitas Scordiscorum*. The city territory of *Bassianae* extended in the north and south to the river Danube, while the western border was the neighbouring *Sirmium* territory in the direction of Jarak-Hopovo. The wider territories of both these cities are characterised by typical Pannonian plains, which are partially interrupted by the southern and south-eastern slopes of Fruška Gora (*Alma Mons*). That area marked by the rivers Sava and Danube and rich in smaller waterways was especially convenient for establishing small rural settlements – *vici* as well as agricultural estates – *villae rusticae*. Thus, in the area of village Hrtkovci, besides the partially explored villa at the site of Vranj, five more villas have been recorded on the basis of surface finds of building rubble and other archaeological material. These are at the sites of Starčevo Brdo, Jarčina (two villas), Vukoder and Simote. The remains of the mentioned villas were positioned on the foundations of earlier settlements from the 1st and 2nd centuries, as has been ascertained for most of the so far investigated villas in the Pannonia province.

Region of Mačva and the Drina Valley

The region of present-day north-western Serbia (Mačva and the Drina valley) is of exceptional importance for studying Roman villas in the area of the Central Balkans. Thanks to the partial archaeological excavations conducted during recent decades, new light has been shed on the antique topography of the region (Vasić 1985, 124-141). This is the area where three Roman provinces, *Pannonia Inferior, Dalmatia and Moesia Superior,* border each other (Popović 1996, 137-142). Thus, the border between Pannonia and Upper Moesia ran along the Kolubara River, while the south-eastern border of Pannonia encompassed Mačva and the area around the Kolubara River. The line of the southern Pannonian border has not been precisely determined. The Dalmatian-Pannonian border could have traversed the Drina River approximately in the region of its tributary, the Drinjača (Dušanić 1971, 546-547). Much of the mountainous region of the Drina valley owed its development to mining and forest exploitation and, in much the same way, Mačva developed as a result of being an intensive agricultural region. This entire area abounded in *villae rusticae*, i.e. agricultural estates. Particularly densely populated was the region toward the Sava River, which is understandable considering the fertility of the land in the area, together with the fact that it gravitated toward *Sirmium* as a great urban centre. In general, considering the distribution of villas and settlements, we have the impression that they were mostly located immediately next to rivers and that to the left and right of the rivers were open areas for cultivation. It is without doubt that certain communication routes also had a significant impact on the location of the villas.

When we speak about villas in this region, two essential questions could be asked. The first is the question of the size of the villas and then the question regarding their ownership. In other words, we still cannot say in most cases what types of properties we are dealing with. It is unclear as to whether they were rather small estates of free peasants or large estates given to the *coloni* to work on. In the present phase of investigation we could assume that large economic estates, like *praetorium fundi* or *praesidium*, existed across the entire Central Balkans region and also in the Mačva region.

It should be taken into account that most of the discovered villas are from the Late Roman times, i.e. the 4th century. It is well-known that large estates with *coloni* were established in the Roman Empire in the 4th century. It is certain that in the 4th century there existed free peasants, independent of large land owners, who did not hold the status of *coloni* (tenant farmers) (Jones 1973, 797). *Libanius* divided villages in Syria in the 4th century into two categories, villages belonging to the great landowners and those divided among small owners (Lib. *Or.* XLVII, 4, 11). There are no direct historical sources for the area of the Central Balkans for the 4th and 5th centuries, but we could assume that the situation was similar to the other parts of the Empire. Such a conclusion is suggested by the data from the time of Justinian who, as part of his legislative activity, paid considerable attention to the protection of small owners from the larger landowners, whilst also recruiting soldiers from their class (Jones, 1973, 780). We will not be able to speak with any certainty about the owners of those villas until systematic archaeological excavations and the analysis of portable material is performed. This will offer a clearer picture of the economic power of the owners and the standard of living in such villas. It should be noted that the colonate system was introduced in the Central Balkans later in comparison to the other parts of the Empire. Consequently, we could assume that the process of tying peasants to the land in this area was applied more slowly and that, in most cases at least, we could expect to see properties with smaller plots of land. Another factor that influenced the rise of the *villae rusticae* in the 4th century was the fact that cities experienced rapid economic decline. This led to the urban population progressively leaving the cities to inhabit rural areas. This process was especially prevalent in the western parts of the Empire (Lewit 2004, 34-37).

In the region of Mačva, which is so far the most thoroughly investigated area in the territory of the *Moesia Superior* province where Roman villas are concerned, it is most probable that a seasonal labour force was employed, especially in the grape picking season (Jones 1973, 792). Such a conclusion is also suggested by an archaeological survey of the sites in Štitar and Kusanje where, besides main residential building for the estate owner, there are smaller structures, huts, in which hired workers may have resided. The system of hired labour is also suggested by the well-known large monetary hoard from Svileuva, in the vicinity of a villa at the site of Kusanje (Petrović 1928-30, 88).[1] The hoard contained coins from the period of Gordian III to Carinus. We could assume, judging by the large amount of money in the Kusanje hoard, that this was an agricultural estate of some considerable size.

---

[1] The hoard was discovered in 1916. 11,000 objects are stored in the National Museum in Belgrade. Later investigations in the 1970s, conducted by M. Vasić and M. Vasiljević from the National Museum in Belgrade, resulted in the assumption that the hoard might have consisted of 16,000 pieces of Roman coins.

One of the investigators of that entire area, M. Vasić, attempted to establish the chronology of those *villae rusticae* on the basis of the surface finds (pottery, coins) and the monetary hoards. He proposed the hypothesis, which we generally accept, that the development of agriculture started in these areas in the middle of the 1st century AD, and in the 2nd and 3rd centuries a larger degree of immigration and development of agriculture, primarily farming, took place. Here we should mentioned the villa at Bela Crkva, where remains of antique structures have been encountered (Šabac u prošlosti I, 75). A well-known hoard consisting of silver jewellery, vessels and money was also recovered from that site (Petrović, 1941, 11-23).[2] Coins from that hoard span the period from Nero to Commodus, so we could classify the villa as one of the earliest, with its date of construction assumed to be the mid 2nd century AD. To the same period could be also dated a villa from Mehovine, where a hoard of denarii dating from Nero to Maximinus I was discovered (Vasić 1913, 226-267).[3] Approximately of the same date is a villa from Banovo Polje, where some pottery finds date from the mid 2nd to the 3rd century (Vasiljević 1980, 208). A villa in Dvojska (Vasić 1972, 62) and a villa from Donje Crniljevo (Vasiljević 1980, 211) most probably date from the middle of the 3rd century.[4] Additionally, a villa in Petlovača (Šabac u prošlosti I, 75) also dates from the end of 3rd and the beginning of the 4th century, based on a discovered monetary hoard at that location dating from the middle of the 3rd to the first half of the 4th century. However, according to the opinion of M. Vasić, most of the recorded villas date from the middle of the 4th century, with some of them inhabited until the first half of the 5th century (Vasić 1985, 124-141). It is without doubt that all the above mentioned sites were connected by a system of communications.[5]

Viminacium and its surroundings

Very little is known about villas in the vicinity of *Viminacium*, the capital of the *Moesia Superior* province, particularly taking into account the importance and position of this city in the Roman Empire. In the course of investigations at *Viminacium*, lasting many decades, villas have not been adequately investigated and presented to the academic audience, despite being very important for the investigation of the economy of the antique city (Fig. 1).

When the city had the status of a *municipium*, its territory covered a larger part of the plain in the lower course of the Mlava River, on the present day Stig plain while, after acquiring the status of a colony, *Viminacium* expanded to cover the entire Stig plain and Veliko Gradište (*Pincum*) and its mine (Popović 1968, 30). Stig is the second largest plain in Serbia, with its northern border the Danube, to the west the Mlava River and in the east and south-east it borders the ranges of the Homolje Mountains (Đokić, Jacanović 1992, 61-110).

Numerous archaeological remains throughout the Stig territory indicate the existence of estates of small landowners (Spasić-Đurić 2002, 44), a fact that is entirely understandable given that the fertile Stig plain was suitable for farming, especially for growing grains. The remains of a few *villae rusticae* have been discovered at various locations within the city ager in the course of archaeological investigations at *Viminacium*: Burdelj, Livade kod Ćuprije, Na Kamenju, Nad Klepečkom, Rit, Rudine and Stig (Jovičić 2012, 378), (Fig. 2). The discovered remains of the villas are only briefly mentioned without any precise description or analysis. There has been a tendency in the recent years among the investigators of the archaeological site of *Viminacium* to carry out more detailed analysis of the mentioned villas, including

---

[2] The richness of the finds and the Illyrian character of certain jewellery pieces confirm the hypothesis that in the 2nd and 3rd centuries there were fewer free land owners.
[3] The hoard contained around 2,000 coins.
[4] 2,657 coin pieces were found in the hoard, from the time of Commodus to Gallienus. Architectural remains have also been discovered.
[5] More details about Roman roads in south-eastern Pannonia and Upper Moesia in a separate chapter of this book.

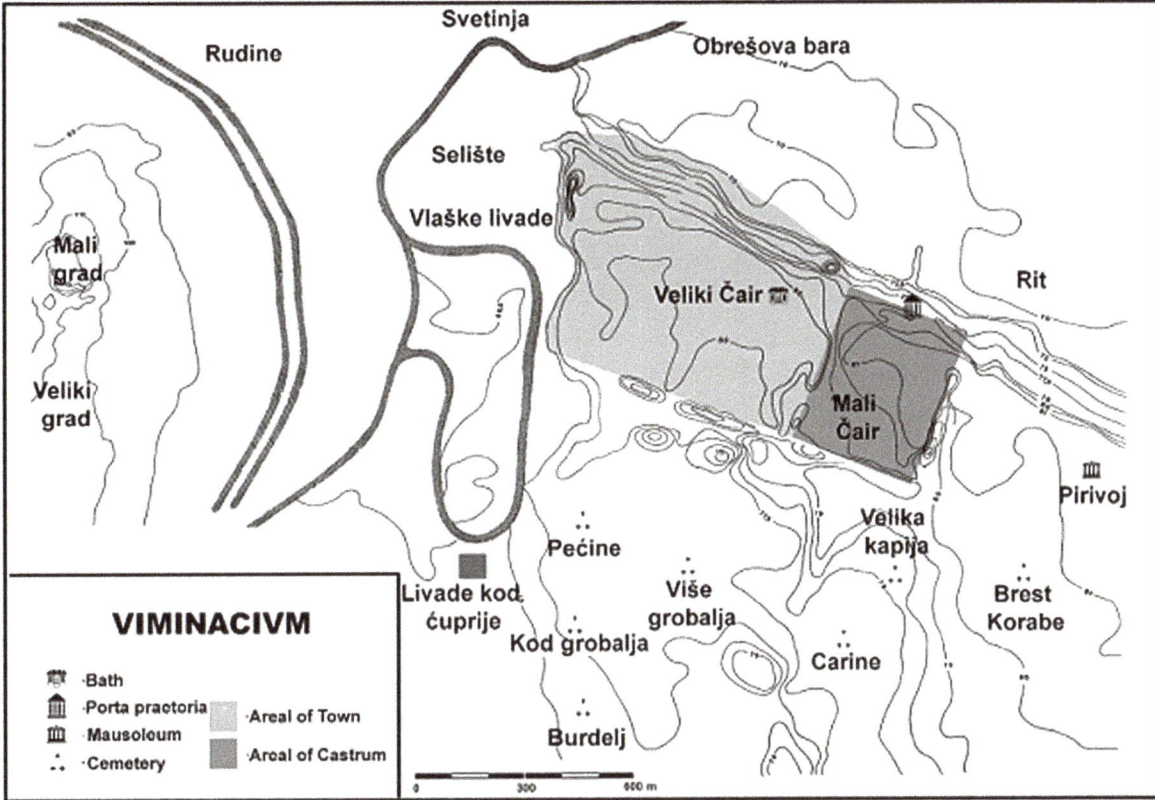

Figure 1. Viminacium, site. (Doc. of the Institute of Archaeology, Belgrade, Project Viminacium)

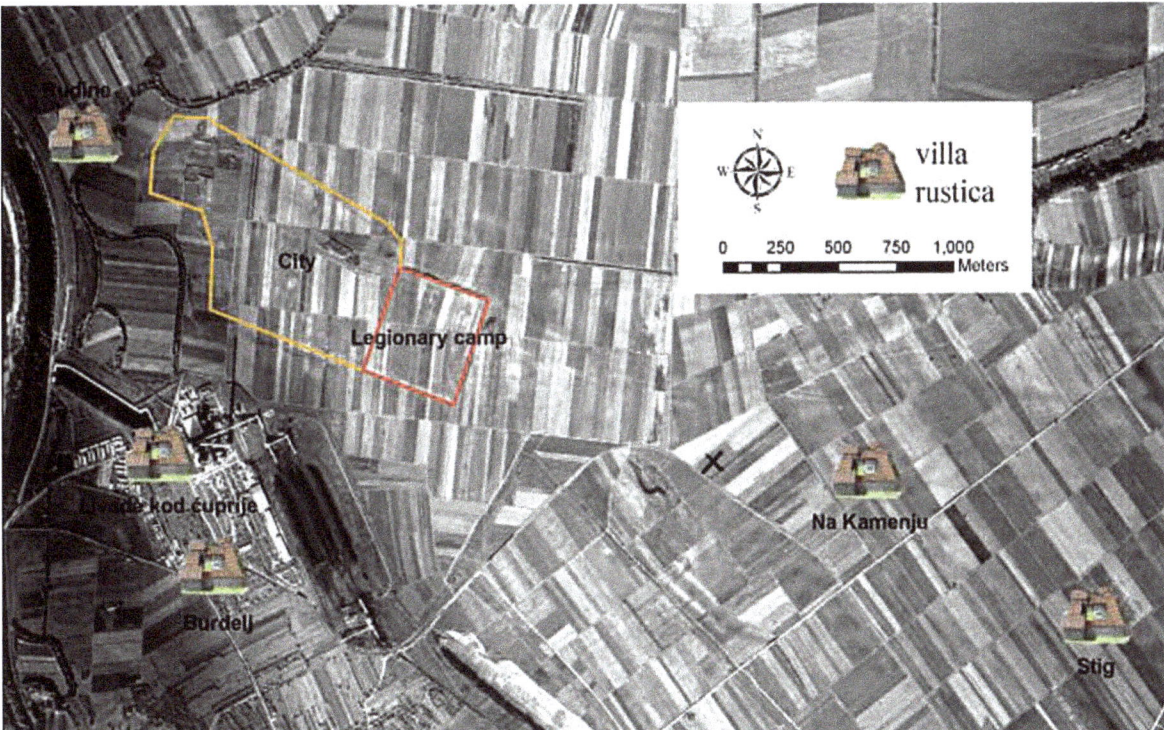

Figure 2. Viminacium, *villae rusticae*. (Doc. of the Institute of Archaeology, Belgrade, Project Viminacium: M. Jovičić)

topographic and typological determinations. However, it seems that some more comprehensive studies are still required.

Naissus and its surroundings

The identification of Roman economic estates, i.e. *villae rusticae*, within the area of the city of *Naissus* and its vicinity poses a special problem. The existence of such agglomerations can only be assumed, considering that no single site identified as a villa has yet been thoroughly investigated (Vinik, Gorica, Bojnik-Direktorovo, Vrbovac-Imanje Pešića, Podrimce-Belije, Ograđe). All these sites are situated near rivers. Their identification as villas is possible only indirectly, on the basis of architectural remains or other archaeological finds. Thus, from the site of Imanje Pešića at Vrbovac come two stone winepresses for pressing grapes (Stamenković 2013, 134-135) that corroborate the importance of viticulture in these areas. A similar press, but of a circular ground plan, was found next to the thermae at Mediana, near Niš. The construction of the villas at Mediana probably started at the end of 3rd century and continued with greater intensity in the 4th century (Petrović 1976, 66), and this information could be used for dating the presses from Vrbovec. Remains of a villa are also assumed at the site near Bojnik. Sondage investigations have revealed a possible room with an apse that could have belonged to a villa. A marble male head, dated to the end of 3rd or the beginning of the 4th century, suggests the possible period of construction of the villa (Jocić 1989, 289-295).

4

Structures for Storing Agricultural Products

Great attention was paid during the entire existence of the Roman Empire to the storing of agricultural products, especially grains, and this was also confirmed some Roman agronomists. Pliny distinguishes two types of large structures for storing agricultural products: *horrea* – massive buildings built mostly of bricks and stone and *granariae* – light structures made of wood. Besides these structures, Pliny also speaks about pits for storing grain – silos, as this was the tradition in provinces on the fringes such as Thrace, Cappadocia, but also outside the borders of the Empire in Barbaricum (Plin., *Nat. Hist.*, XVIII, 73). Both types of warehouses were used to store all agricultural products but particular attention was paid to the storage of grains, being the most important food. G. Rickman, in his comprehensive study on granaries, speaks about two types of granaries, civil and military (Rickman 1971, 1-12). It seems to us that this distinction is quite adequate, so we are going to hold on to such distinction in the ensuing text.

Civil *horrea* were sturdy, massive structures with an upper floor and a gable roof. The interior space of one type of these granaries was divided by rows of pillars and, in such a way, the possibility of penetrating damp was reduced, while interior of the other type was divided by transverse walls.

The structures had thick walls in order to provide the best protection from possible fire or theft. Their windows were narrow and placed high above the ground and there were strong locks and bolts on the doors. The placing and removal of products was carried out by hand, so it is assumed that large *horrea* employed a large number of workers. Approach ramps were placed in front of the entrance so that loaded carts could come as close as possible. Remains of civil *horrea* have been found in all parts of the Empire, within urban structures, at large country estates but also within military camps, where they played an important role in supplying the army with food.

We have discovered more about public *horrea*, their function, and the transportation of agricultural products thanks to the preserved historical sources. Imperial rescripts collected in the *Codex Theodosianus* date from the late 4th century and the beginning of the 5th century. They provide detailed surveys not only of large *horrea* in the capitals, Rome and Constantinople, but also information about the numerous civil storehouses scattered throughout the provinces of the Empire (Rickman 1971, 163). Despite the fact that this legal act concerns the Late Antique period, G. Rickman reasonably assumes that changes in the organisation of civil *horrea* are insignificant in comparison to the early Empire (Rickman 1971, 163-164).

Greatly significant for the territory of North Africa, i.e. Egypt, as the most important breadbasket of the Empire, are the preserved papyri, which cover the period from the first Ptolemies to the Byzantine period. In these documents could generally be found data about the organisation and transportation of grain in Egypt (Rickman 1971, 298-306).

Within the territories of the Roman provinces of Pannonia and Upper Moesia, structures have been encountered which could be identified as civil *horrea*: Sremska Mitrovica (*Sirmium*), Maskar near

Topola, Prijevor near Čačak, Gamzigrad near Zaječar, Ravna near Knjaževac and Mediana near Niš, (Map 5).

Supplying the Roman army stationed on the Danube Limes, but also deeper in the hinterland, required the construction of structures intended for the storing and preservation of food which could satisfy the needs of army garrisons for a specific period of time. Such military granaries (*horrea militaris*) constructed within army camps were most often of a rectangular ground plan and a variety of sizes, depending on the stationed army units for which they were intended. These structures were mostly of sturdy construction, raised off the ground and sometimes reinforced with counter-forts. Few *horrea* have been identified within army fortifications along the Upper Moesian Limes: in Sapaja, Čezava (*Novae*), Boljetin (*Smorna*) and Veliki Gradac (*Taliata*), (Map 5).

All those storehouses for grain, either of civilian or military character, encountered in the Roman provinces in the territory of Serbia are not distinguishable, regarding their structure or purpose, from numerous structures of the same type constructed throughout the Roman Empire. They confirm that the careful supplying of grain, *cura anonnae*, was an important factor in the Roman state throughout its entire existence.

Civil *horrea*

Regarding the Roman provinces in the territory of present-day Serbia, we can select only a few discovered rather large civil *horrea*, which we will be discussed in this work in more detail: two in *Sirmium* in the province of *Pannonia Inferior* and Maskar near Topola, Prijevor near Čačak, Gamzigrad near Zaječar, Ravna near Knjaževac and Mediana near Niš in *Moesia Superior*. Something that is common to all the mentioned *horrea* is that they were built during a relatively short period of time, during the reign of Diocletian and Constantine I. Additionally, their structure and method of construction are so similar, particularly the granaries in Maskar and Gamzigrad, that the impression is that the same master masons designed and built them both. Also very similar in shape and method of building are two *horrea* from the Kosovo region: in Sočanica (*Municipium* DD) (Čerškov 1970, 15-21) and in the vicinity of Peć (Srejović 1982, 39). The similar time of construction and appearance of these granaries corresponds to the new political and economic changes that were taking place at the time of the tetrarchy. These monumental granaries indicate a well established system of collecting and distributing food in the hinterland of the Danube Limes. Their construction could, perhaps, be related to the introduction of new taxes, *annona militaris*.

Sirmium: Two civil *horrea* have been discovered within the city territory of *Sirmium*, one was located in the central zone of the city, in the vicinity of the public baths, and the other was in the immediate vicinity of the southern city wall, not far from the Sava River.

Horreum at locality 30

A monumental *horreum* in the central section of the city was discovered in the 1960s (Popović 1962, 111-119; Popović 1965, 111-114). The structure is situated at locality 30, in the central zone of the city and near the public baths. It is a building with a portico and is a massive structure with an external wall. The internal space was divided by rows of pillars (five in each row) into five aisles. The massive walls are supported on the outside and the inside by pilasters in such a way that each external pilaster corresponds to an internal one. Millstones that have been found inside the building also indicate the purpose of the structure.

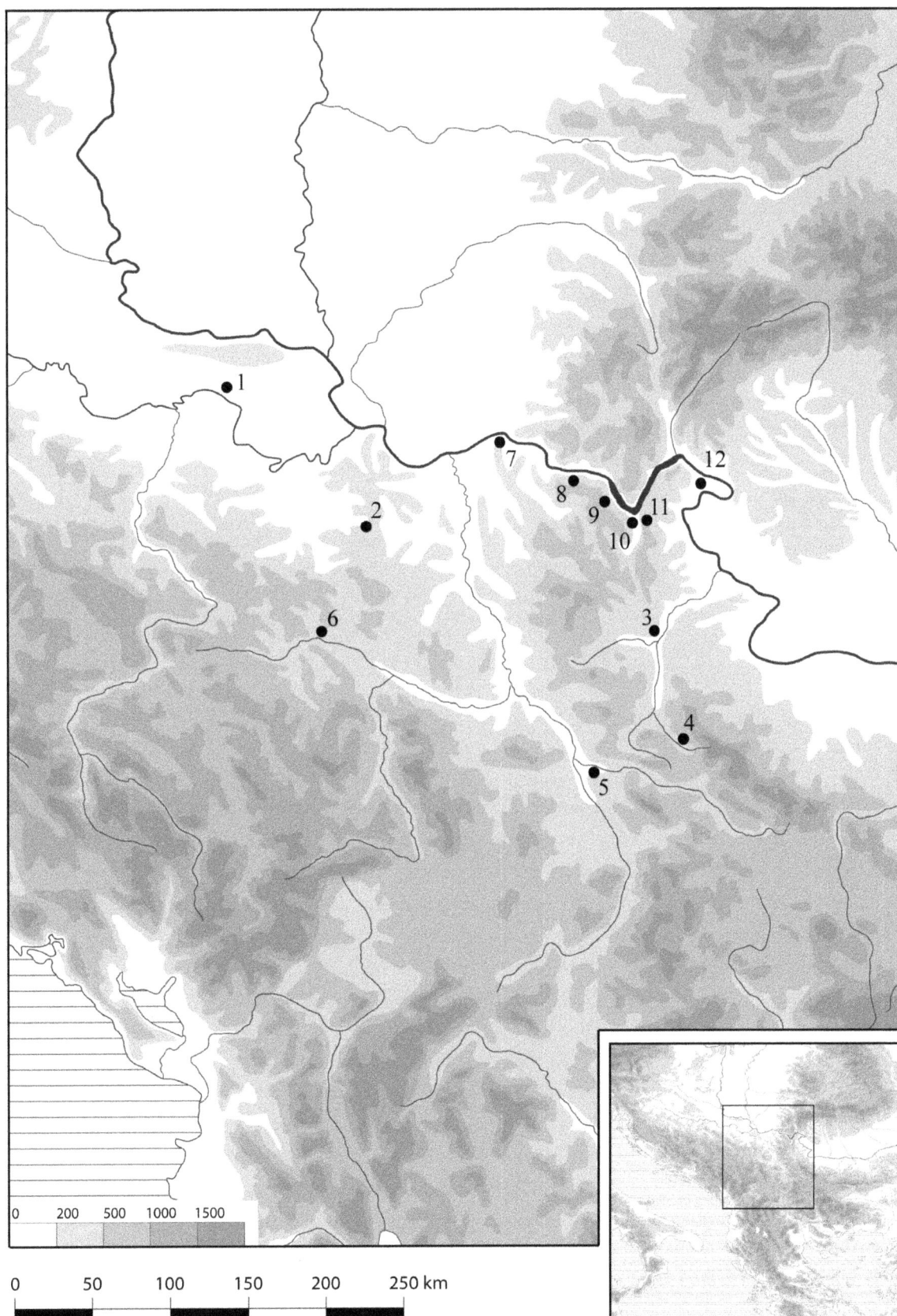

Map 5. Roman granaries in the territory of present-day Serbia: 1. Sirmium, Sremska Mitrovica; 2. Maskar, Topola; 3. Gamzigrad, Zaječar; 4. Ravna, Knjaževac; 5. Medijana, Niš; 6. Prijevor, Čačak; 7. Sapaja, Ram; 8. Čezava; 9. Boljetin; 10. Veliki Gradac; 11. Porečka Reka; 12. Kurvingrad

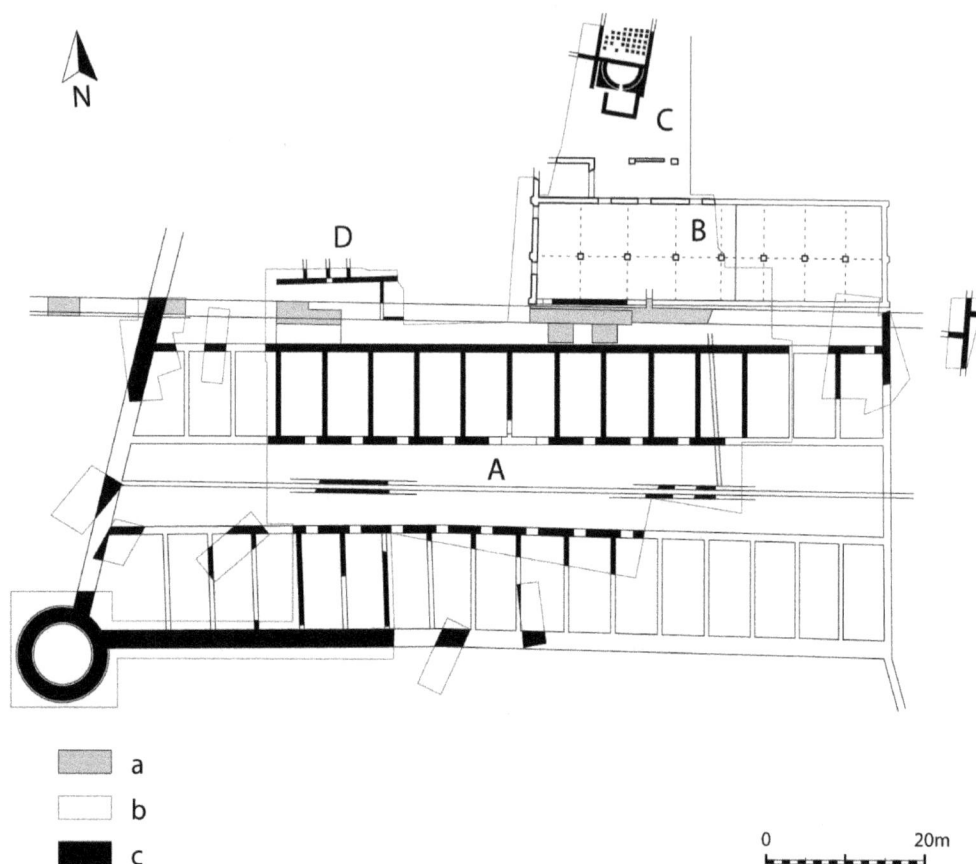

Figure 3. Sirmium, *horreum* at locality 31. (Drawing by M. Jeremić)

Horreum at locality 31, next to the southern city wall

Next to the southern city wall of antique *Sirmium* yet another complex of buildings intended for storing grain, *horreum*, was constructed. It was located in the immediate vicinity of the representative monumental structures – the imperial palace and the hippodrome (Fig. 3). Most of this complex was discovered in the course of rescue archaeological excavations at the beginning of the 1960s[1] and sometime later at the beginning of 1970s.[2] Two structures (denoted in literature as structures A and B) can be distinguished within this complex, surrounded by the strong walls of the southern defensive zone (Bošković, *et al.* 1973, 193-200; Duval, Popović 1977, 29-73).

Structure A: the need for new storage facilities dates from the time of the tetrarchy, at the end of 3rd and the beginning of the 4th century, when *Sirmium* became one of the most important cities of the Empire. A new city wall was shifted about 35 meters to the south. At the same time, the new wall was used as the southern and western walls of the new *horreum*, denoted in literature as structure A. It is a monumental granary, around 85 meters long and around 33 meters wide. It consists of two tracts with a paved yard between them, where a channel was installed along the longitudinal axis for collecting rain water. Both tracts are of an approximately identical width (around 10 m) divided into identical spaces, thus forming 33 separate rooms. The structure was built in the *opus mixtum* technique, i.e. of broken stone and layers of brick between the courses of stone. The positions of the entrances of the opposite rooms of the southern and northern tract correspond with each other, thus making possible the quick loading and

---

[1]   Rescue excavations at locality 31 were conducted in 1961 and 1962 by the Institute of Archaeology in Belgrade and in the following year the Regional Office for the Protection of Cultural Monuments, in Novi Sad and the Museum of Srem, in Sremska Mitrovica were also included.
[2]   Joint Yugoslav-French investigations of locality 31 in 1973 were a continuation of earlier rescue archaeological investigations carried out in 1961-1962.

unloading of goods. The doorposts were built of bricks, without the use of stone. Somewhat worn-out mortar floors with sporadic finds of a gravel substructure have been encountered in all the investigated rooms. The main, and only, approach to the granary was on the eastern side, facing the imperial palace. This fact, as well as the fact that the long northern wall isolated the building from the neighbouring structures, led its investigators to assume that this complex of *horrea* did not have a public character; rather that it was a structure which may have been an integral part of the imperial palace complex (Jeremić 1993, 103).

Structure B: was leaning on the original massively built southern wall from an earlier building phase dating from the 2nd and 3rd centuries and was, according to the investigators, used for a certain period of time as its southern wall (Bošković, *et al*. 1973, 196). Later, the new southern wall of the structure was built after the original city wall was damaged. The interior, with a series of brick-built square pillars along the longitudinal axis, was divided into eight identical compartments by transversally placed wooden partitions. The height of these partitions was limited by storage conditions and technical restraints during the loading and unloading of grain. In the northern section of the building was a portico, and at its western end was added a rectangular room, which was an integral part of the building.

Maskar near Topola: The remains of a Roman settlement were discovered in the 1950s at the site of Crkvine, in the village of Maskar, near Topola in central Serbia (Srejović 1982, 35-43). The almost completely preserved foundations of the structure made possible the reconstruction of its appearance and purpose and also explains, to a great extent, the character of the settlement itself. The structure is of a rectangular shape and consists of one large room (Fig. 4). Two rows of eight pillars divide the room into three aisles. One meter thick walls rest on ample foundations made of stone rubble and mortar. The external facade of the structure is divided by pilasters of the same size as the pillars in the interior. As only the building foundations are preserved, it is uncertain what the floor was like and where the entrance to the building was located. Conclusions could be drawn about the walls, only on the basis of the finds of stones and bricks in the cultural layer. It is most probable that the commonly used method of building such structures was applied, with the main building material being half-dressed stone with layers of bricks in-between. Preserved remains of tegulae and carbonised timber posts in the cultural layer suggest that the roof was of a gable type and covered with tegulae. Judging by the preserved architectural elements, the thickness and depth of the foundations, the walls being reinforced with pilasters and the pillars in the interior, the structure most probably had an upper storey.

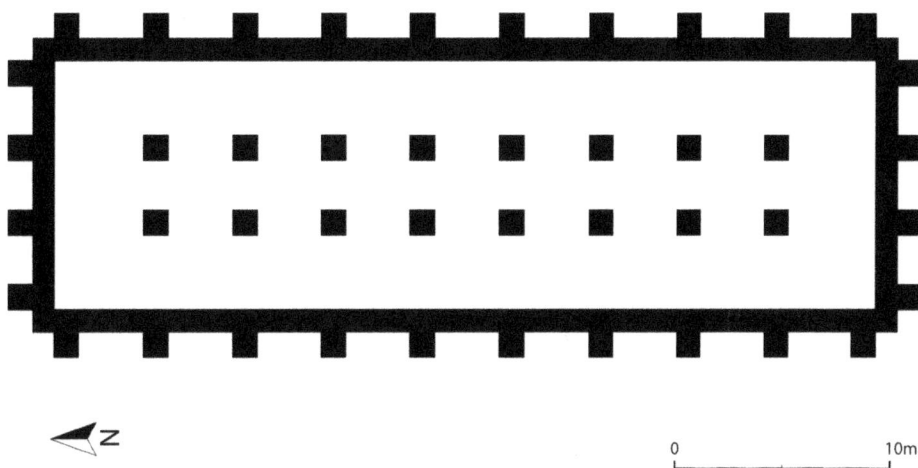

Figure 4. Maskar, near Topola. Plan of the *horreum*. (Altered after: D. Srejović, 1983)

The period of construction and the use of the structure could be determined on the basis of coins discovered in its interior (42 pieces). With the exception of one specimen from the time of Gordian, all other pieces date from the 4th century, i.e. they were minted in the period from Licinius and Constantine I to Theodosius I (Srejović 1982, 37). These finds suggest that the date of the structure's construction is most probably the second decade of the 4th century and the date of its destruction was the end of the same century, as the latest found coin was minted in 383. It is also most likely that this structure, like most of the others of the same purpose, was destroyed during the time of the Gothic invasion of the Balkan Peninsula after the battle of Adrianople. The preserved remains of singed roof beams in the cultural layer speak in favour of such a conclusion.

Gamzigrad near Zaječar (*Romuliana*): The remains of a structure were discovered at the site of Malo Gradište, to the west of the palace in Gamzigrad, in the course of archaeological excavations at the beginning of the 1980s (Srejović 1083, 52-53). The structure is built to a rectangular plan (Fig. 5). Its interior is divided by two rows of eight pillars into three aisles. It was solidly built with thick walls resting on top of large and deep foundations made of stone rubble and mortar. The facade was divided by pilasters. The walls are preserved up to a height of 2.5 meters and reinforced on the inside with a wide socle. The walls were built from half-dressed stone with layers of brick in between. Remnants of arches are preserved in a few places on the northern wall. The entrance to the building, 2.5 meters in width, was in the eastern wall. The width of the foundations, the walls strengthened with pilasters and pillars, probably joined by cross-vaults, indicate that the structure had an upper storey. Windows were probably located between the pilasters. The roof was most probably of the gable type, as with most buildings of this kind, and covered with tegulae. This structure resembles, in its construction, numerous granaries built in the Roman provinces at the transition from the 3rd to the 4th century (Rickman 1971, 163-209). They were all built on a rectangular plan and divided by two rows of pillars into three aisles. They have also been recorded in the surroundings, in the previously mentioned Maskar near Topola, in the province of *Dardania* in Sočanica and in the suburbs of Peć in Kosovo. The similarity of all these structures in appearance as well as in their method of construction is certainly the result of new economic measures introduced by Diocletian. The size of the granary at Gamzigrad indicates the possibility that it was the collection point for grain from neighbouring farms and, at the same time, the location from where further distribution would have been carried out, possibly to the military fortifications on the Danube Limes.

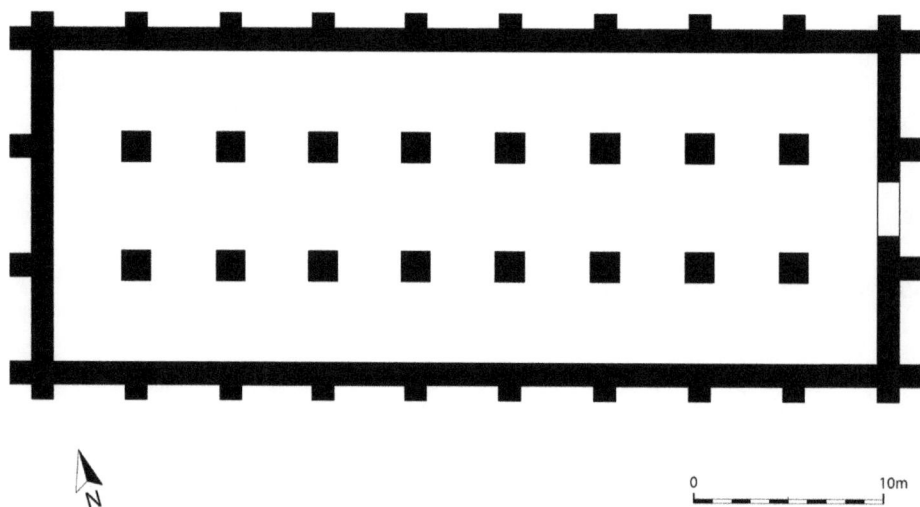

Figure 5. Gamzigrad, near Zaječar. Plan of the *horreum.* (Altered after: D. Srejović, 1983)

Ravna near Knjaževac (*Timacum Minus*): The earliest and most important traces of a Roman presence in area of eastern Serbia were recorded at the site of Ravna, near Knjaževac. Continuous systematic archaeological excavations have been carried out in recent years in the military camp of *Timacum Minus* (Petrović 1995, 19-59; Petrović 1997, 115-131). A relatively large structure (30 x 15 m), was discovered to the north of the *via principalis*, within the camp walls. The structure had been used as a *horreum* in Late Antiquity, in the 5th and 6th centuries, as confirmed by the finds of pithoi and the carbonised remains of grain (Petrović 1995, 42).

***Mediana* near Niš:** The *horreum* at the site of *Mediana* near antique *Naissus* is located to the west of the building with a peristyle. Investigations of the structure started in 1936 (Братанић 1938, 199-204), but not until archaeological excavations conducted at the beginning of 1980s was the ground plan of the building completely explored (Čerškov 1986, 41-43). It is a rather large structure of an elongated rectangular ground (Fig. 6). The entire granary was longitudinally divided by two rows of 11 pillars made of stone and brick. The structure was built of stone rubble joined with mortar, with brick used on the external sections of the walls. The floors are mostly destroyed in all sections of the granary and traces of a mortar floor over a substructure of pebbles are only partially preserved.

The entrance to the granary was in the southwest and a portico with columns was erected in front of it. Two separate rooms opened to the right of the portico. Across from them were another two separate rooms, added to which were six rectangular rooms in the western wing. By all appearances, this tract had an upper storey, as suggested by the remains of a staircase in front of one of the rooms. The purpose of these rooms could not be determined with any certainty, but it is assumed that they were lodgings for the personnel carrying out a diverse range of activities in the process of the collection and distribution of grain (Petrović 1994, 42). Traces of an intensive fire, which destroyed the structure, were recorded all over the building area.

The remains of 37 huge pithoi (around 2 meters tall), which were half buried in the ground, are preserved between the pillars dividing the interior of the largest longitudinal room of the building into three aisles. Next to the western wall of this long room were basins of up to 1.40 meters deep; one in the middle was of a circular shape and the two on the sides were of a square ground plan. The meticulously polished interior surfaces of these basins was made of hydraulic mortar, suggesting that large quantities of liquid (oil, wine) could have been safely stored in them.

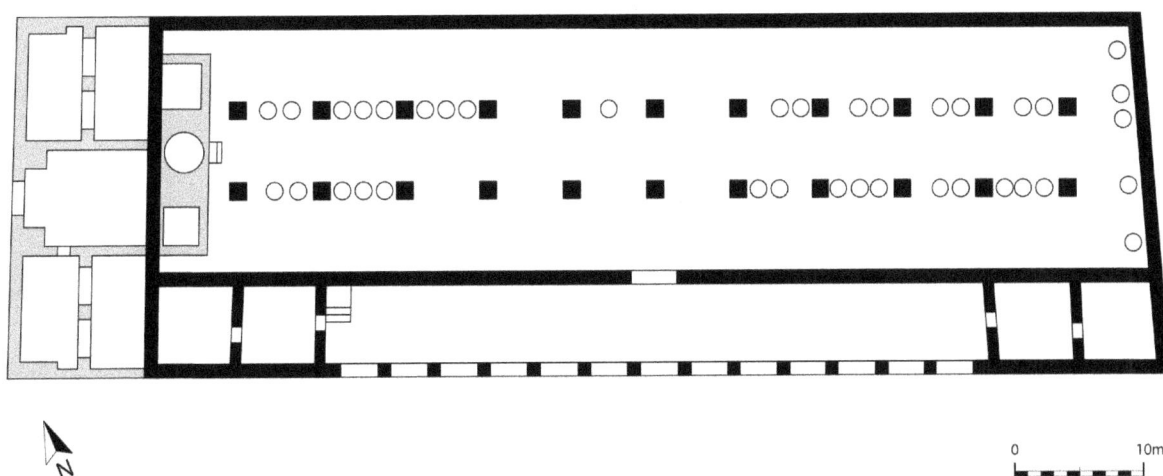

Figure 6. Mediana, near Niš. Plan of the *horreum*. (Drawing by G. Milošević, in: P. Petrović, 1994)

Inside the building were discovered the remains of decorative architectural elements: fragments of marble columns and bases and marble plaques with channels that were used as wall facing. Fragments of flat glass, which most probably originated from the windows, have also been registered.

Taking into consideration the size, capacity and architectural structure of the granary at *Mediana,* it can be assumed that not only grain, wine and oil was stored there, but also other food provisions. Archaeological material discovered during excavations is not very abundant, except for a large number of iron wedges, clamps and nails used to join together the wooden roof structure. The remains of a cart (*plaustrum*) with one preserved iron-tyre for a wheel were found in the immediate vicinity of the building. The discovered section of the granary was, according to the opinion of the investigators, in fact a cellar for processing and storing grain and wine, above which was the ground level with a floor at the same level as the mouths of the pithoi, then above that was a loft space (Čerškov 1986, 46).

One rather interesting find are the two fragmented altars discovered next to the western *horreum* wall (Mirković 1982, 360-366). According to the opinion of T. Čerškov, one of the investigators, these *arae* were in secondary use, horizontally perforated and most probably used as presses for wine or oil. As both *arae* are votive in character and the inscription on one of them has a dedication to Jupiter, Čerškov considers that they were used in the time of Christianisation (Čerškov 1986, 43). Contrary to that opinion, P. Petrović thinks that the altars were not in secondary use but that, by all appearances, they were originally erected inside the granary at the location where they were found (Petrović 1994, 45). Specifically, it was frequently the case that small shrines and altars were organised in food storehouses so, in accordance with this, these altars may have been a specially arranged shrine. The dedication to pagan deities on the altars is not an obstacle for dating them to the time of Constantine. It should not be forgotten that this was the period of religious syncretism and that Christianity was not yet dominant or the only allowed religious concept. It should also be mentioned that other dedications in inscriptions, on sculptures and mosaics from *Mediana*, still had a pagan character.

The size of the granary and the solidity of its structure indicate a well organised agricultural production on a large scale in this area, as confirmed by the capacity of the storage space. The three building phases encountered in the course of archaeological excavations speak to the organised use of the structure throughout an extended period of time.

The structure was probably destroyed during the Hunnic invasion in 441-443, when Roman *Naissus* was destroyed, as along with most of the cities and fortifications to the south of the Sava and the Danube in the one-time Upper Moesia province. A monetary hoard (273 pieces) discovered in the western section of the building confirms the assumption regarding the date of destruction. The results of investigations have revealed that the structure was not renovated in the later, Paleo-Byzantine period.

Military *horrea*

Apart from the major supply centres in which food was kept for further distribution, forts along the Danube Limes had to have their own buildings intended for food storage for the soldiers stationed in them. According to Tacitus, the *horreum* of each camp was constructed in such a way as to hold a year's supply for the soldiers stationed there. Although this data relates to fortifications in Britain during the second half of the 1st century AD, it can easily be presumed that the same principle was valid throughout the Empire (Tac. *Agric.* 1, 21). Such measures were needed in cases of inconvenient circumstances along the Roman limes or bad weather conditions, which could cause problems with food transportation. Several granaries that we can call *horrea militaris* along the Danube Limes of

Moesia Superior were located within fortifications of different sizes and shapes: in Sapaja near Ram, Čezava (*Novae*), Boljetin (*Smorna*) and Veliki Gradac (*Taliata*). Forts of smaller dimensions did not have enough room for such buildings (Map 5).

Sapaja near Ram: The Danube river island of Sapaja, which was located near present day Ram on the right bank of the Danube, no longer exists. The objects discovered on this site belong to the period from the early Roman Empire to the medieval period.[3] Previous researchers believed that near the site of Ram was located one of the crossings over the Danube, where Trajan transferred his troops into Dacia. A multitude of bricks with stamps of the cohorts who participated in Trajan's Dacian war have been discovered, along with bricks with stamps of the Legion *VII Claudia* (Mirković 1968, 100).

In front of the western wall of the later fortifications, at a distance of 15.2 m, there was a small *horreum*, rectangular in base, made of stone and mortar (Fig. 7a). Only two bases of small ceramic bowls, of Roman and Sarmatian production, were found inside the granary (Dimitrijević 1984, 29-64). At the section of the Danube Limes in the province of *Moesia Superior*, the most similar analogy to our facility is an almost identical structure in the *castrum* of Boljetin, although it is larger in size, with 8 rooms. Lj. Zotović, the researcher of the site, dated the *horreum* to the 1st century AD (Zotović 1984, 211-226). It can be assumed that the warehouse in Sapaja was built just a few decades later, because as well as the formal similarity between these two structures in support of this dating, there exists other data that speaks about their similarities. Namely, after the conquest of *Dacia*, at the beginning of the 2nd century, the Danube was no the longer frontier, although people remained in most of the fortifications on the Danube. Near Ram, the crossing over the Danube was still functioning, but on the island a new fort was not built, only a small *speculum* and *horreum*. Such a fortified structure had the function of an observation point or bridgehead that was supposed to protect the Danube crossing. The situation later changed, especially after Dacia was abandoned in 272, when the island of Sapaja regained its strategic importance. There was no logical reason for the storehouse being constructed outside the walls of the fortress, especially after the abandonment of the province of *Dacia*.

In that period, the *horreum* on Sapaja was too small to satisfy the wheat requirements of the late antique fortress, which was among the largest in this sector of the Danube Limes. The protection of food supplies was a foremost task of the Roman army. These reasons, point to the assumption that the *horreum* must belong to an earlier phase of fortification on the island of Sapaja.

Čezava (*Novae*): The *castrum* in Čezava (*Novae*) was located 18 km downstream from the town of Golubac. Systematic excavations of the structure started in the sixties.[4] Within the explored part of the fort, the walls and buildings inside the fort which allowed the differentiation of several phases were discovered (Vasić 1984, 91-122). Besides the other buildings within the fort, a square granary in the area west of the *principa* was also discovered (Fig. 7b). Inside the building there were three rows of pillars which divided the space of the granary. The phase of the *castrum* in which the *horreum* was constructed, based on the findings of ceramics, fibulae, coins and other archaeological finds, has been dated from the end of the 2nd to the second half of the 3rd century (Vasić 1984, 100).

Boljetin (*Smorna*): The fort in Boljetin (*Smorna*) is located between the fortresses of *Novae* and *Taliata*, and was one of the largest in this part of the Danube Limes (Kondić 1974, 53-57). In the north-eastern part, which was the economic part of the fort, a small rectangular *horreum* was discovered (Fig. 7c). It

---

[3] Small-scale archaeological excavations on the island began in 1966. Systematic excavations were entrusted to the Institute of Archaeology SASA in 1967, in collaboration with the National Museum in Vršac and lasted until 1970, under the direction of Prof. Jovan Kovačević.
[4] Systematic excavations were entrusted to the Military Museum in Belgrade, in 1965, and lasted until 1970.

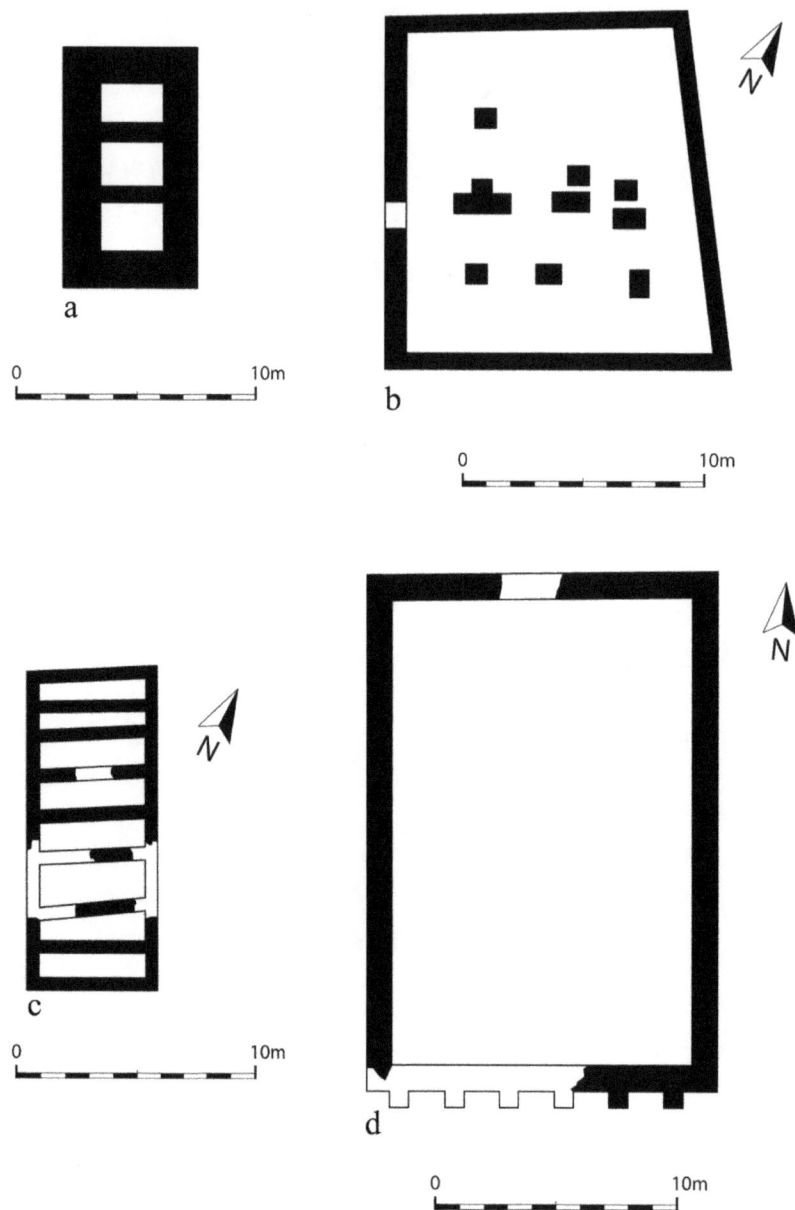

Figure 7. a) Sapaja, near Ram. Plan of the *horreum*; (After: D. Dimitrijević, 1984); b) Čezava (*Novae*), near Golubac. Plan of the *horreum*; c) Boljetin (*Smorna*). Plan of the *horreum*; d) Veliki Gradac (*Taliata*). Plan of the *horreum* 4th century. (After P. Petrović, M. Vasić, 1996)

was built on the older cultural layer, made of stone and mortar. The walls were plastered inside, while the floor was constructed of pebbles from the river over which mortar had been poured. It was partitioned on the inside with eight walls. A small number of archaeological finds, mostly fragments of pithoi where grain was stored, were found within these buildings. Due to the small number of these fragments, it is uncertain whether the grains stored in the pithoi or were deposited directly into the partitions. This *horreum* has been dated to the Flavian phase, like the aforementioned *horreum* in Sapaja, near Ram (Zotović 1984, 217-219).

Veliki Gradac (*Taliata*): The *Taliata* fort is located at the crossing from the upper to the lower Iron Gate gorge, not far from the mouth of Porečka Reka. Located on the bank of a wide river, the fort played an important role in the defence of the province of *Moesia Superior*, preventing incursions from *Dacia*. The earliest fortification dates from the second half of the first century and is the oldest *horreum* of the three from that time which have been found near the north gate of the fort (Fig. 7d.). Investigations of the oldest buildings for storage have not been completed, so only its 21 m long east wall, with six well-preserved pilasters, are fully explored. The wall is made of stone and mortar. The dating of this object was made on the basis of the preserved archaeological material: Roman pottery, Dacian pottery and coins from the 1st century AD (Popović 1984, 265-282).

As with most of the fortifications at the Iron Gate Limes, the Roman fortification of *Taliata* lost its significance as a defensive point on the border after the conquest of *Dacia*, but archaeological material shows that life continued in the camp during the 2nd century. This leads to the assumption that the *castrum* at that time functioned as a supply centre with storehouses.

In the 3rd century, after the abandonment of *Dacia*, there was a renewal of the fort. At this time a new granary was built. The interior of the space is divided into two longitudinal areas, with a wall of about 0.85 m thickness. It is probable that this building, like the previous one, had a single storey structure. It was mostly built above the old building. Several millstones were found in the area, which could characterise this as a *horreum* complex.

Another object with the same purpose was also found at the site. It was a building with a porch facing the street. This *horreum* has been dated to the early Byzantine fortress of the 6th century.

This whole complex of grain storage was built along the north gate of the fort. It hasn't revealed traces of a stone threshold, adjusted to accommodate a horse-drawn carriage, which indicates the possible existence of a river port in this area; given that the main land access was most likely on the western side (Popović 1984, 279-280).

5

The Main Roman Routes in the Pannonian-Balkan Region

The strategic importance of the Pannonian-Balkan region is shown by the most important roads that served the Balkan Peninsula during the ancient period. This geographical area is characterised by having a network of roads adapted to the configuration of the terrain. All the major routes went through the valleys of the major rivers. The first of them went through the valleys of the Sava, Danube, Great and South Morava rivers and the Vardar, in the central region of the Balkan Peninsula, linking different geographical regions.

Roman military penetration along the Sava valley was of historical importance as it was the most convenient communication toward the East. In the process of conquering Pannonia, the Romans used well-known prehistoric migration and commercial routes. First contacts of the Romans with lower course of the Sava River date from the time of Octavian's campaign in Illyricum, in 35-33 BC, that reached as far as *Siscia* (Dio. *Cass.* XLIX 36).[1] The period of establishing Roman administration included setting up new towns, rural settlements and lines of military fortifications – *limes*– and it was necessary to connect all this with the new network of roads. It was particularly important to establish connections with the home territory in Italy.

Communications in Pannonia are known on the basis of antique itineraries where the most important roads with names of settlements and distances from each other described. Within the system of Roman roads, *Sirmium* was one of the most important crossroads in the Roman Empire (Map 6). In the itineraries the city is marked, from which the total distance from Aquileia in northern Italy to Nicomedia in Asia Minor (*Itin. Anton.* 124, 2) was measured. It is not known when this road network was created. It is possible that some roads were built in the time of Augustus. The road running along the Sava valley toward Italy must have existed during the Dalmatian-Pannonia resurrection, when many troops were transported to the theatre of operation in present-day Srem in Vojvodina and in Bosnia. We may assume that it was constructed in the time of the Roman wars in Pannonia in 34-33 BC or 12-11 BC. There is, for the time being, no direct evidence concerning the construction of these roads. The earliest known milestones from the vicinity of *Sirmium* are not earlier than the time of Marcus Aurelius, i.e. the 160s AD.

Villas and smaller rural settlements that were situated to the east and northeast of *Sirmium* were not recorded in the itineraries, so their names remain unknown. Their existence is indicated by some discovered monuments, many Roman tegulae and traces of walls. Thus, three miles to the east of *Sirmium*, in the area of the village of Šašinci, the road passes through the site of Crepovac, where two milestones were discovered. One is from the time of Marcus Aurelius, from the year 161 (*CIL* III 10615; *Sirmium* I no. 92), and the other from the time of Septimius Severus, from the year 198 (*CIL* III 10616; *Sirmium* I no. 93). They both record a three mile distance, corresponding to the distance

---

[1] Information from the antique writer Cassius Dio (Dio. Cass. XLIX 36), indirectly suggest that this campaign went further to the east, as far as the confluence of the Sava and the Danube. Works concerning this problem were mostly based on this source: Mirković, Miroslava, *Sirmium – Its history from the I century to 582 AD, Sirmium I*, Beograd: 1971.

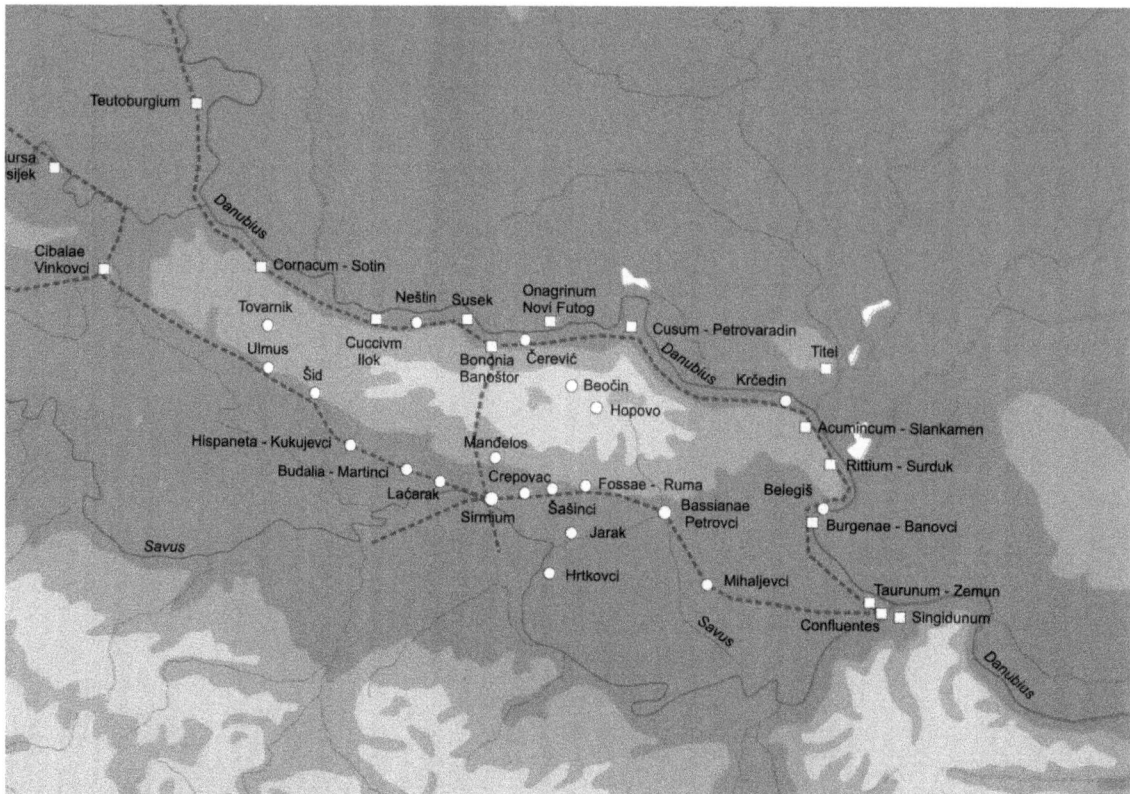

Map 6. Roman roads in Srem. (After: M. Mirković, 2006)

between *Sirmium* and the present-day site of Crepovac. The territory of *Sirmium* extended in the east to the border of the territory of *Bassianae*, which obtained its urban status in the 3rd century. Before that, this settlement near the present-day village of Petrovci was included in the peregrine community of the Scordisci in eastern Srem. *Sirmium*, is represented in *Tabula Peutingeriana* as an intersection of roads. It was connected with *Aquileia* and northern Italy, via *Mursa* and *Cibalae* on one side, and in the east, with *Singidunum*, at the mouth of the Sava River, on the other. Additionally, it was connected to the fortification of *Bononia* on the Danube, with the legion camp in *Aquincum*, upstream near Budapest, and downstream with *Taurunum*, at the location of present-day Zemun (*Taurunum*), where the headquarters of the Pannonian fleet was located.

We also know from Roman itineraries about the communication route connecting *Salona* and *Sirmium*. The road crossed the Drina River at a spot called *Ad Drinum*, located in present day Zvornik. The road then followed the right bank of the Drina River up to present day Banja Koviljača, as is confirmed by the remains of the road that were visible until the middle of the last century (Vasiljević, Trbuhović 1985, 35). From there the road turned northward, crossed the Mačva region and continued on to *Sirmium*. On that road was the station of *Gensis*, located close to Lešnica. The exact location is not certain but, according to researchers who, in the 1980s, investigated this area, there is a strong probability that stations (*mansio*) existed in Lešnica, Runjani, Loznica and Koviljača (Vasiljević, Trbuhović 1985, 36).

From *Taurunum* and *Singidunum*, the road connects the military fortresses and settlements on the limes of the province of *Moesia Superior*. The first station in the province of *Moesia Superior*, west of *Singidunum*, was *Confluentes*, located on the south bank of the River Sava (in the present-day Belgrade suburb of Železnik). East of *Singidunum*, on the western part of the Danube Limes, a neighbouring settlement and military fort were established. Between the confluences of the Sava, Mlava, and Danube rivers, spanning approximately 50 Roman miles, lay the urban settlements of *Singidunum*, *Margum* and *Viminacium* (Maps 7, 8). *Aureus Mons*, lying between *Singidunum* and *Margum*, also probably had the status of a city.

Map 7. Roman road Singidunum-Viminacium. (Doc. of the Institute of Archaeology, Belgrade, Project Viminacium)

Map. 8. Roman road Singidunum-Viminacium. (Doc. of the Institute of Archaeology, Belgrade, Project Viminacium)

The remains of *Singidunum* are located beneath the present-day Belgrade. Initially, it was probably a military fort of one of two legions that began to built infrastructure on the Moesia Limes, legion *IV Scythica* or legion *V Macedonica*. As a legionary camp (*castrum legionis*), *Singidunum* was first referred to by Ptolemy in the middle of the second century, while its military company is quoted as the *IV Flavia legion*. This legion arrived in the region of the Danube around 86 AD, but was moved to *Singidunum* later, during the reign of Emperor Trajan (Mirković 1968, 40, 41). Fortifications on the upper urban plateau of the Belgrade fortress at Kalemegdan were constructed as a permanent camp of the *IV Flavia* legion, stationed there from the second decade of the second century, and up to the last decade of the fourth century AD. Remains of the *castrum* have been partially uncovered and excavated over many years of archaeological investigation of the Belgrade fortress.

The civilian territory of *Singidunum* was mentioned in the second half of the fourth century, with Aurelius Victor as *ager Singidunensis* (Aur. Vict. *De Caes.* 44). Its occupied area and extent is not known, but it is supposed that in one period, certainly before 333 AD, it extended to *Aureus Mons* (near the present-day village of Seona), 25 Roman miles to the east. Near Seona, bricks were found with the inscription *ripa Singidunensis*, while not far away, in the town of Smederevo (*Vinceia*), a brick was found with the inscription *ripa Viminacensis*. On the basis of these finds, it can be assumed that between these two present-day communities of Seona and Smederevo lay the border between the towns of *Singidunum* and *Viminacium*. To the west, the civil territory of *Singidunum* extended to the *Confluentes* stop. Settlements that lay within the civilian territory of *Singidunum*, mentioned in itineraries, are *Mutatio Ad Sextum*, *Castra Tricornia* and *Ad Sextum miliarem*. All these settlements lay on the road to *Viminacium*.

The most important road on the Balkan Peninsula, named *Via Militaris*, started from the southern end of the regions of Pannonia and the confluence of the Sava and Danube rivers, where *Singidunum* was situated. It ended at Thessaloniki Bay in the city of Thessalonica. Here it connected with the major road of the Roman period, *Via Egnatia*, which was constructed in the 2nd century AD, and started from the port of Durres (*Dyrrachium*), in today's Albania, went through Macedonia to Thessalonica Bay then along the northern coast of the Aegean Sea to Constantinople (Map 9). The Morava-Vardar route that went across the middle of the peninsula, between the Balkans and Rhodope to the east and the Dinara and Shar mountains to the west, using the natural advantages that they offered, branched out in all directions. Thus, in the Pannonian area, the Morava-Vardar route connected to all those roads that were along the Danube, from the upper Danube region, through the Pannonian Plain and up to *Singidunum*. In this way, the roads of the Pannonia and the Danube region further increased the importance of the Morava-Vardar route. Some branching of smaller roads was caused by unfavourable geographic factors. East of the Morava-Vardar road, *Naissus*'s road separated from the *Via Militaris*, went through the Nišava and Maritsa Valleys and continued to Constantinople and Asia Minor. On the eastern side of the Moravian-Vardar road was the road along the Danube, the Iron Gate route which, at the Pontes fortress, crossed the Danube over Trajan's bridge and continued on to the Carpathian regions.

The whole of this network of communication through Pannonia and the Balkan Peninsula shows how the area of the Middle Danube and Morava valley formed a well-connected entirety. This fact has largely contributed to the area becoming a focal area with a significant density of population. This area is still more important bearing in mind the navigable streams that formed the Danube, as the main navigable river, and then its tributaries: the Sava, the Tisza and the Morava, where Roman ships carried a variety of goods as well as people. Also along the rivers, especially the Danube, were military ships whose job it was to protect the Danube Limes from possible attacks.

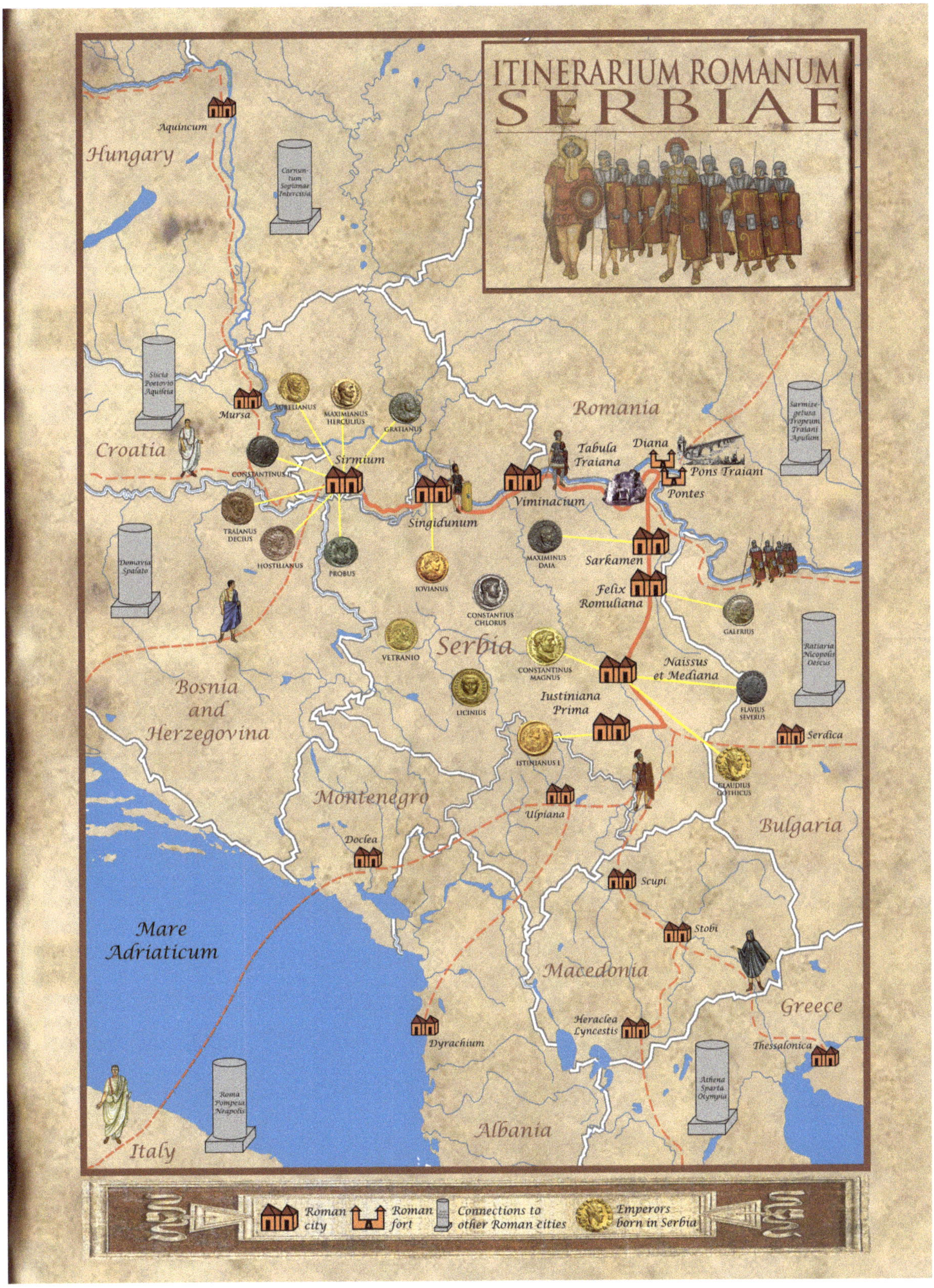

Map 9. Roman roads on the Balkan Peninsula. (Doc. of the Institute of Archaeology, Belgrade, Project Viminacium)

6

Food Supply and Transport in the Province of Moesia
Superior

The question of supplying food has not been studied enough in Serbia, and therefore the results gained are very modest so far. In this sense, the chapter of this book could represent an introduction to the further study of the supply and transportation of food. In the current state of investigations most information about supply relates to the Roman army, so we will devote this chapter of the book to the system of supplying Roman army stationed along the Roman limes on the Danube in the Upper Moesia.

During the past few decades, the question of supplying Roman troops was mostly studied by Petar Petrović (Petrović 1981, 53-62; Petrović, 1984, 285-291). Since historical evidence about the supply of Roman troops along the Danube limes, but also in the hinterland of the province, is poor, archaeological data has gained in importance. By relying on this data, we shall attempt to reconstruct the methods of supplying and transporting goods in this region, which was of the highest importance during Roman times. We will deal with the supply of garrisons and units stationed in their permanent camps. Actually, supplying units whilst on the march and in hostile territories represents a study of a different kind and could be the subject of study of some work in the future. Where the limes of *Moesia Superior* are concerned, two aspects can be analysed:

- the first concerns geographical regions and is directly related to the relief of the terrain:
  a) the area from *Singidunum* to the Iron Gates, b) the Iron Gates themselves and c) the area downstream from the Iron Gates;
- the second concerns troop supply according to rank – legions or auxiliary troops.

Where geographical aspect is concerned, one can clearly distinguish three regions along the Danube limes, each of which possesses its own specific features (Map 10).

The first region includes the territory from *Singidunum* (Belgrade) to the *Cuppae* (Golubac), at the entrance of the Iron Gates. This area is plain, convenient for agriculture and the concentration of large military formations. In this territory, both legions of the main defence of the *Moesia Superior* were stationed (in *Singidunum* and *Viminacium*). In other words, the nucleus of defence was concentrated exactly where it was easy to supply large numbers of troops and, furthermore, part of the supply was conducted by the legions themselves. Of main importance was the fact that the area was of agricultural character. Around each and every legionary camp there was *territorium*, land given to legions so that they could fulfil their basic needs of food production and building material. *Prata legionis* was also mentioned in sources and inscriptions, and was used by a legion for its own purposes. It remains unclear, however, whether *prata legionis* represents the same thing as *territorium legionis* (Mocsy 1972, 133-168; Zaninović 1985, 63-79; Mason 1988, 163-189).

From a series of possible explanations given by Bohec, one can single one out which is also expressed by Schulten (Bohec 2000, 219), that the *prata legionis* included pastures, forests and fertile fields, clay

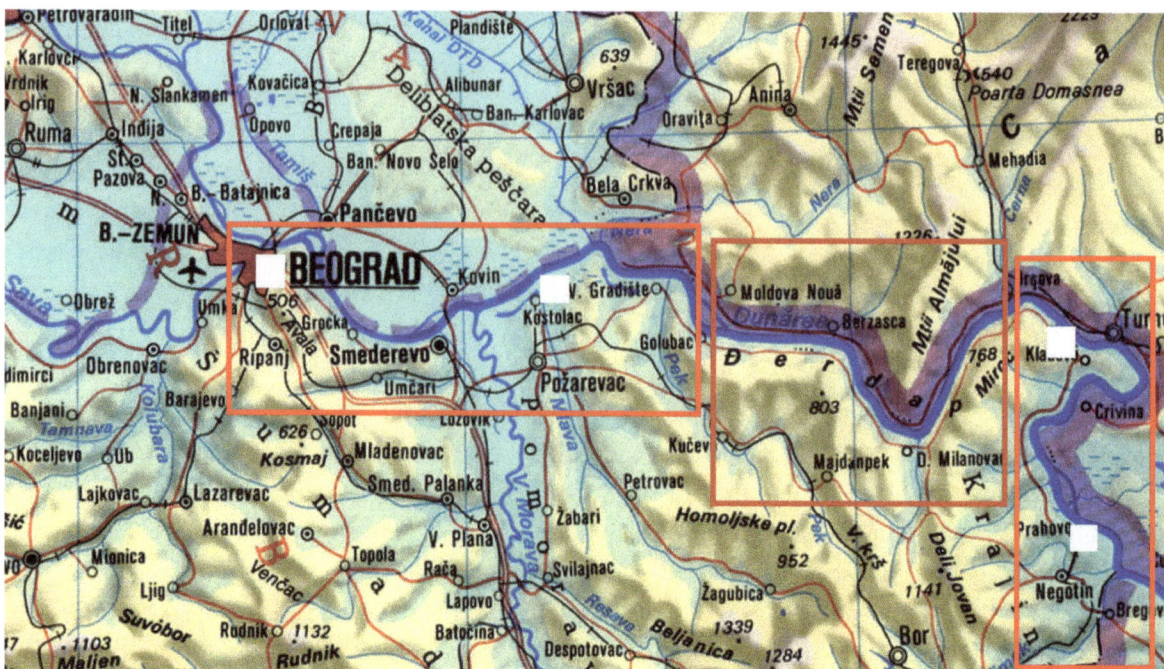

Map 10. Geographical regions along the Danube limes

deposits etc., while *territorium* includes the complete area under the legion's supervision and which practically formed a military administrative unit. In this sense, a *territorium* would include *canabae* and workshops which were built outside the camps. Finally, although *canabae* were settlements of civilians and *territorium* could spread around civilian settlements, these were strictly under military government.

The problem of military territories is most of all present in bordering areas, such as in the limes along the Rhine and the Danube, where numerous camps were built with large numbers of soldiers who needed to be supplied with food, weapons, equipment and other goods. In this sense, the question of the area covered by a *prata legionis* or a *territorium legionis* arises. In the first place, the size of the legion's territory depended on the number of soldiers for which supplies were needed, and for which an exercising area was also needed. According to one milestone, it is known that the *Prata legionis* of the legion *III Macedonica*e in Asturia measured about 560 km2 (Mason 1988, 164). *Prata legionis* did not supply soldiers only with grain. Each legion had a squad of about 120 cavalrymen plus additional mules and oxen used for the transport of legionary supplies. Food for animals was no less a problem. It was partly solved by the fact that the military also controlled numerous pastures which were usually several hundred hectares. According to some authors, livestock could have numbered up to several thousands of animals: riding horses, workhorses, pulling animals, mules, oxen and food animals such as sheep and goats (Zaninović 1985, 67).

Livestock was the responsibility of special services in particular legions *pecuarii* and *veterinarii* (*CIL* III 11215; *CIL* XIII 8287). Agriculture and stock-breeding were also a part of the non-military activities of the soldiers and surely reduced the need for supplies and the cost of the supply process (Tac. *Ann.* XIII, 55). Grain, as a main food, was mostly grown in legionary fields. Soldiers could also have bought food from the numerous land-owners of the farms surrounding *Singidunum*, *Margum* or *Viminacium*.

The close proximity of rivers was a great advantage for all the camps built along the Limes, since it made fishing possible. Still, *annona militaris* and the principle of obtaining legionary supplies from civilian sources in the form of taxes collected in goods was of main importance, because it was not possible to produce enough food from the *prata legionis* alone.

The second geographic region includes the Iron Gates. In this area, military units up to the rank of cohort were stationed. The gorge itself did not represent an area adequate for agriculture, so, apart from Porečka reka, the needs of these units had to be satisfied by transporting food from supply centres situated mostly in the hinterland (*Horreum Margi*). A smaller number of soldiers within such a unit was an advantage, but the size of fortifications (*quadriburgium, speculum*) represented a problem, since they, apart from some exceptions, were very small and did not possess a granary or any other similar building suitable for keeping food supplies for a longer period of time. This led to regular, short term, food supplying operations, in which supply centres were permanently engaged, while each fortification was supplied periodically.

It should be added that the vicinity of the great river enabled fishing as a form of food supply for the crews of the fortifications. Iron hooks and weights for fishing nets are often found in the settlements and forts on the Danube limes dating to the period from the 1st to the 4th century, indicating favourable conditions for fishing: *Singidunum, Saldum, Pontes*, Rtkovo-Glamija (Jeremić 2009, 178, fig. 86, cat. 556-569; Gabričević 1986, fig. 22/9; Krunić 1997, cat. 327-329).

The third geographic region included the area downstream from the Iron Gates, in which, again, larger fortifications were built (*Statio Cataractarum Dianae, Pontes, Egeta*). This area was not suitable for the long-term stationing of legions, since around these military camps there were not enough fields for crop growing. Units up to the size of a *cohors militaria* could have possessed an equivalent of a *territorium* around their camps.

Speaking about other aspects of supply, it is certain that they depended on the rank and size of a military unit. Due to them having a large number of soldiers, legionary units were supplied with much more food and other goods needed for active service. Legionaries, compared to auxiliary soldiers, were also entitled to a larger amount of provisions.

The system of supplying the military with food raises many questions concerning mostly whether food was brought from distant areas or from areas in the vicinity, from the local population. There is no doubt that olives, olive oil, garum, better quality wine and tropical fruits were brought from distant areas because amphora-finds throughout the Empire give testimony to this fact. The Danube Basin of *Moesia Superior* had been supplied with products from West and East Mediterranean that evidenced with transport containers like vessels and *amphorae* from the great number of sites in this region (Bjelajac 1996, 9-118).

The question of the supply strategy also arises, i.e. whether the military took part in tax collection (most of all in goods collected as taxes), bought directly for its needs, or had contracts according to which its needs were satisfied. No matter how food was obtained for each Roman soldier, it is most likely that the basic food and drinking supplies were the same throughout the Empire. Data from written sources or archaeological finds from other provinces could help in building a complete picture of food supplying in the province of *Moesia Superior*. Egyptian papyroi from the 6th century give data about the daily needs of an average Roman soldier from about 360. Daily supplies of a soldier included: 3 libras of bread, 2 libras of meat, 2 pints of wine, 1/8 pint of oil (Jones 1973, 629).

Under the principate the regional distribution of food was administered by the province's *procurator Augusti*. Provincial governors, who were primarily responsible, were connected to military procurators (*frumentarii*). A *frumentarius* was, at first, a soldier who had the duty of supplying the military with grain. Sometimes governors had to intervene against malfunction or corruption in the system of collecting and transporting grain to the Roman army (Tac. *Agr*. 19. 4). In time, their reputation of *frumentarii* became so bad that, in the 4th century their titles were changed from *frumentarii*, (*pestilens frumentariorum genus* – known as "filthy merchant kin" by the local population) to *agentes in rebus* (secret military intelligence) (Nelis-Clement 2000, 118).

In the territory of *Viminacium*, a monument was discovered with the name of a *frumentarius* (Mirković 1986, no. 47, 84). One can still not say whether he was connected to the grain supply to the soldiers in this area or if he played the role of a spy sent from Rome.

Two interesting findings are the altars discovered by the western entrance of the *horreum* in *Mediana* near *Naissus*. One of them is a votive character, dedicated to Jupiter. An inscription allows us to discover more about the supply process in the territory of the province of *Moesia Superior* (Petrović 1994, 42). It is known that the military units of the 4th century who were scattered though the provinces regrouped into smaller mobile detachments, *comitatenses*, and that they were not stationed in one camp as at the time of the Early Empire. The system of supply from the state storehouses, coupled with a complex bureaucratic procedure, required that the units be stationed near larger towns where food and other military supplies were stored. The supply of these mobile detachments was the responsibility of officers – *primipilares*, while the whole organisation consisted of a mixed composition of personnel, civilians (*susceptors, actuarii*) and military persons (*optiones, trubuni*). The civilians, *actuarii*, were under the control of a military commander – *magister militum*. The tasks which were performed in the *horreum* by the tribune Aurelius Ampelius are not specified in the inscription, but according to P. Petrović, it is probable that he was responsible for measuring and distributing the wheat (Petrović 1994, 44).

It is known that *horrea* were exposed to various dangers such as fires and pillage, and that altars were often erected in them. Usually these were dedicated to the *genius* to Jupiter, Silvanus, and other. We can, therefore, assume that smaller sanctuaries and altars existed in almost every storehouse. It is understandable, then, that altars from Mediana could belong to a specially arranged space-sanctuary, in particular, if one bears in mind the quality and enormous size of the *horreum* of *Mediana*.

The dedication to the pagan gods on the altars of *Mediana* does not present an obstacle for dating them to the period of Constantine the Great. What is striking is that other dedications in the inscriptions, on marble and bronze sculptures and mosaics in *Mediana*, have a clearly pagan character. Since the time of Edict of Milan, the pagan religion was not persecuted for a long time. It was a period of religious syncretism.

The *horreum* of *Mediana* certainly stored, in addition to wheat, wine and oil, other products which could be needed in a big town such as *Naissus*. In any case, we are dealing with a storage of great capacity and an attractive appearance which occupied the whole ground floor (the floor made of thicker boards was certainly on the level of the opening of the pythoi that have been found in it). The *horreum* lasted for a longer period of time (three building phases have been identified).

While discussing the Roman supply system and transporting goods, D. Breeze tried to give an answer by stating a hypothesis about four methods of food supply:

1. the cities transported the goods requisitioned from them to the army; 2. the cities employed contractors to transport the goods; 3. the army collected the goods from the point of origin; 4. the army employed contractors to transport the goods (Breeze 2000, 60).

When supplying Roman fortresses along the Limes the province of *Moesia Superior*, there is an opinion among authors who dealt with this problem that such supply was pretty much organized from other towns in the hinterland of the province. *Horreum Margi* could have represented such an important point for gathering and distributing food, most of all grain, owing to its position on the main crossroad, which made access to important centres within the province easy, as well as to the fortresses along the Danube limes. Therefore, it is not strange to think that *Horreum Margi* was in charge of supplying troops along the limes. On the other hand, it is certain that in military camps, or in their vicinity, there were storage buildings, mostly granaries, but also for other supplies intended for the nourishment of the soldiers.

The quantity of food to be stored depended mostly on the size and number of soldiers stationed within a camp, but also on the structure and durability of the food being stored. According to P. Petrović, the number of soldiers stationed along the Iron Gates limes between Sapaja (*Lederata*) and Karataš (*Diana/Caput Bovis*) was 2000-3000 (Map 11), (Petrović 1981, 54). Still, even with that number of soldiers stationed in the camps, the quantity of food which was kept was much greater than the needs of each and every soldier and it was, therefore, necessary to build bigger storage buildings in different locations. Granaries must have existed in all legionary camps that supported smaller forts along the Danube limes. Such legionary camps were in *Singidunum* (*IV Flavia*) and *Viminacium* (*VII Claudia*). The question of river ports on these locations arises as well. Geophysical surveys of *Viminacium* offered plenty of data about the position of the *principium*, buildings and barracks inside the legionary camps. However, without excavations, neither of these can be designated as a *horreum* at the moment.

Buildings discovered at the mouth of the Porečka reka offer some more data about the supply problems along the limes in the province of *Moesia Superior*. The site is situated in a very convenient position, in the vicinity of one of the biggest camps of the Danubian limes – *Taliata* (Veliki Gradac), which had

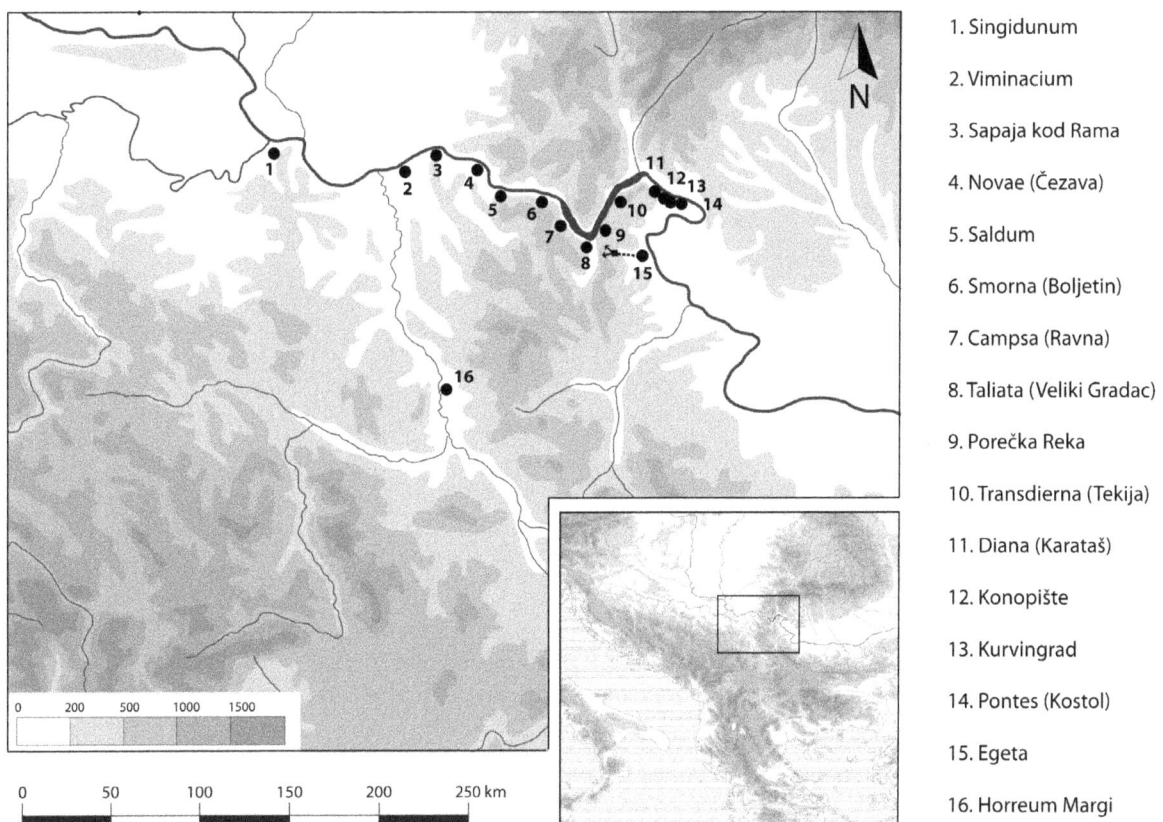

1. Singidunum
2. Viminacium
3. Sapaja kod Rama
4. Novae (Čezava)
5. Saldum
6. Smorna (Boljetin)
7. Campsa (Ravna)
8. Taliata (Veliki Gradac)
9. Porečka Reka
10. Transdierna (Tekija)
11. Diana (Karataš)
12. Konopište
13. Kurvingrad
14. Pontes (Kostol)
15. Egeta
16. Horreum Margi

Map 11. Roman forts along the Danube limes

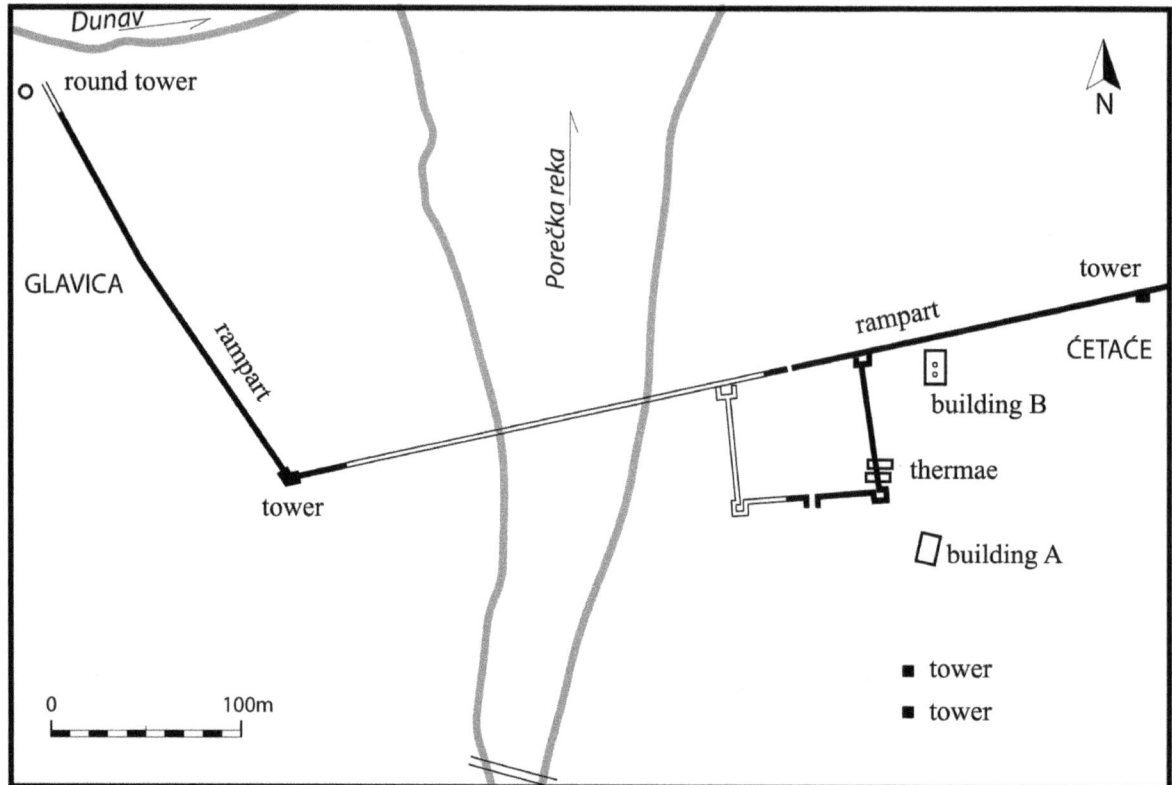

Figure 8. Porečka reka, plan of fortifications. (Altered after: P. Petrović, 1981)

soldiers stationed permanently throughout the Roman and Early Byzantine periods. At the same time, Porečka reka represented an important crossroad on this part of the limes. There was a road which led towards the east, over Miroč and a station called *Gerulata*, to *Egeta* and then connected to the Lower Danube valley, going around the cataracts of the Iron Gates (*Tab. Peut. segm.* VI). The road towards the south lead to the Timok valley. It is most likely that there lay the border of the two Late Antique provinces: *Moesia Prima* and *Dacia Ripensis* (Mirković 1981, 93).

The mouth of the Porečka reka was closed with a stone wall, while on the right hand river bank, there were two rectangular towers (Fig. 8). The most interesting features are two broad buildings of approximately the same size. Building A was made of bricks and stones, with no inner walls, and had a broad entrance facing the south, while building B was made of stone, with two pillars in its interior (Fig. 9). The building was filled with huge amounts of debris, with bricks on which traces of fire were visible. Shards of larger pottery vessels were also found, used for transporting and storing food: pithoi and amphorae. Metal objects were also numerous: three bronze bells, a sickle, an axe, a bigger iron spoon and other tools.

Inside this complex, a *quadriburgium* was erected close to the wall which closes the river valley. On the south side there was a broad main entrance, while there was a narrower one in the north, towards the Danube. No objects or other archaeological finds were discovered within the fortress, except for a large amount of roof-tiles next to the eastern wall, which could indicate the existence of an object close to this side. Sporadic amphorae fragments are the only archaeological material discovered inside the fort's walls.[1]

---

[1] Since the western wall could not be detected and since there was no archaeological material or cultural layers, it was presumed that the river destroyed most of the fort.

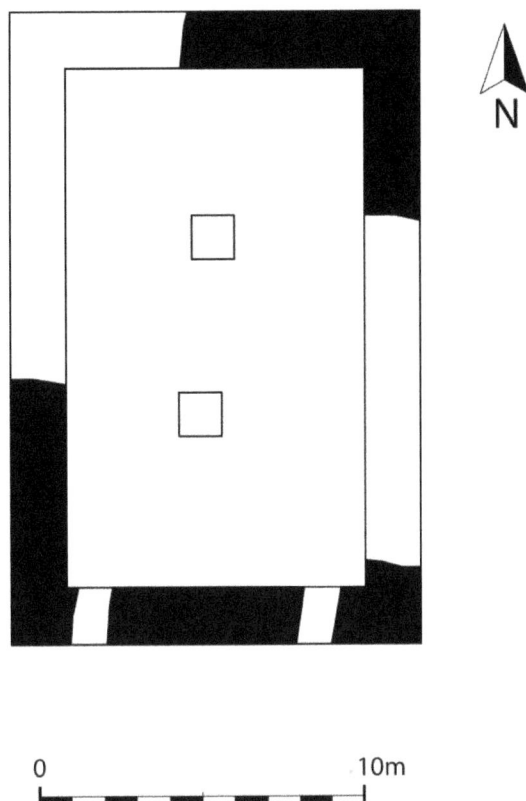

Figure 9. Poreča reka, *horreum*. (Altered after: P. Petrović, 1981)

Regarding historical context and the changes which took place during the Late Antiquity, it is possible to determine the function and chronological frame of the objects described above. The objects A and B can be dated to the first half of the 4th century, which is supported by coins of Constantine, Constantius, Valens and Valentinianus (Petrović 1981, 57). Such a conclusion is also supported by the fact that there are no older building phases of these objects, nor later reconstructions of the same. The fortress was most probably built earlier, during Diocletian's great building activity and his attempts to consolidate the limes throughout the Empire.[2] Still, archaeological research[3] conducted at this site showed that, during the second half of the 4th century, the fortress lay in ruins, since in its southeaster part, thermae were built on the tower (Petrović 1984, fig. 6). Although the building period of the thermae is not certain, it is possible to determine its period of collapse, since a smaller hoard was discovered in a soot layer on the thermae. The youngest of the coins were those from 378 (Petrović 1981, 58). This date can be considered as *terminus ante quem* for its dating.

Reforms of Diocletianus also regarded the question of military supply. The construction of a building related to supplying happened simultaneously with the introduction of military taxes (*annona militaris*). In imperial edicts which regard these questions, the supply and distribution of food was organised by *primipili*, comissary officers for whole sections of the frontier garrisons (Jones 1973, 626-627). They were in charge of the storehouse outside the military camps, which represented supply centres from which food was distributed. Some of these storehouses were located in the neighbouring towns, at greater or smaller distances from the border. There were also other supply buildings, representing isolated fortified centres on the border itself (Rickman 1971, 264). It was most likely that the mouth

---

[2] One should also mention Diocletianus' travels along the Iron Gates in 294, from Singidunum to Ratiaria and further on down the Danube. The building activity was confirmed on numerous inscriptions discovered in forts along the lower Danube valley, erected most likely in the period from 298 to 299.
[3] Field surveys of the site began in 1962 and a systematic excavation took place between 1967 and 1970. The excavation was conducted by D. Vučković-Todorović.

of the Porečka reka represented such a supply centre from which further distribution was done. This conclusion is supported by the position of the fortification close to important military camps along the Danubian limes. Apart from that, the buildings discovered definitely had an economic function as well. According to its plan, building B could have been a granary, most likely also building A. Sporadic finds of amphorae fragments in the inside of the fortress, with no dwelling traces, indicate food storage. In the Roman Empire, examples are known of storage buildings surrounded by walls (Rickman 1971, 266-267, fig. 66).

Two other sites are considered to have been logistic centres in the Danube limes in *Moesia Superior*: Kurvingrad and Konopiste near Kostol (*Pontes*). There is very little archaeological data for either of these sites. At the site Konopiste, 3 km upstream from Trajan's bridge and the fort *Pontes*, foundations of irregular rectangular buildings were discovered (Fig. 10). These buildings were made of stone and mortar. A small number of archaeological finds, mostly amphorae shards from the 1st and 2nd centuries AD, were found within these buildings, as well as a well preserved sestertius of Nerva from 97 AD that provided chronological data (Popović 1996, 103).

The site Kurvingrad, which is today under water, was located one kilometre downstream from Konopište. At the excavated area, buildings used for storing grain and other goods were discovered. The dimensions of the building could not be determined due to erosion. A few finds included amphorae shards, also from the end of the 1st and the beginning of the 2nd century AD (Trbuhović 1986, 59-61).

These two buildings represented a unique complex erected by the Romans on the Danubian terrace in the area from Konopište to Kurvingrad. The remains of these buildings indicate that there was a granary in this area along with other buildings used for storing food, as well as barracks for the soldiers. Amphora shards, as well as coins, indicate dating from the end of the 1st to the beginning of the 2nd century AD, actually a time when Trajan's bridge was built and when accommodation and food supplies were needed for its builders. Since most of them were brought from different parts of the Empire and were stationed here only temporarily, the buildings in which they dwelt were not of a permanent

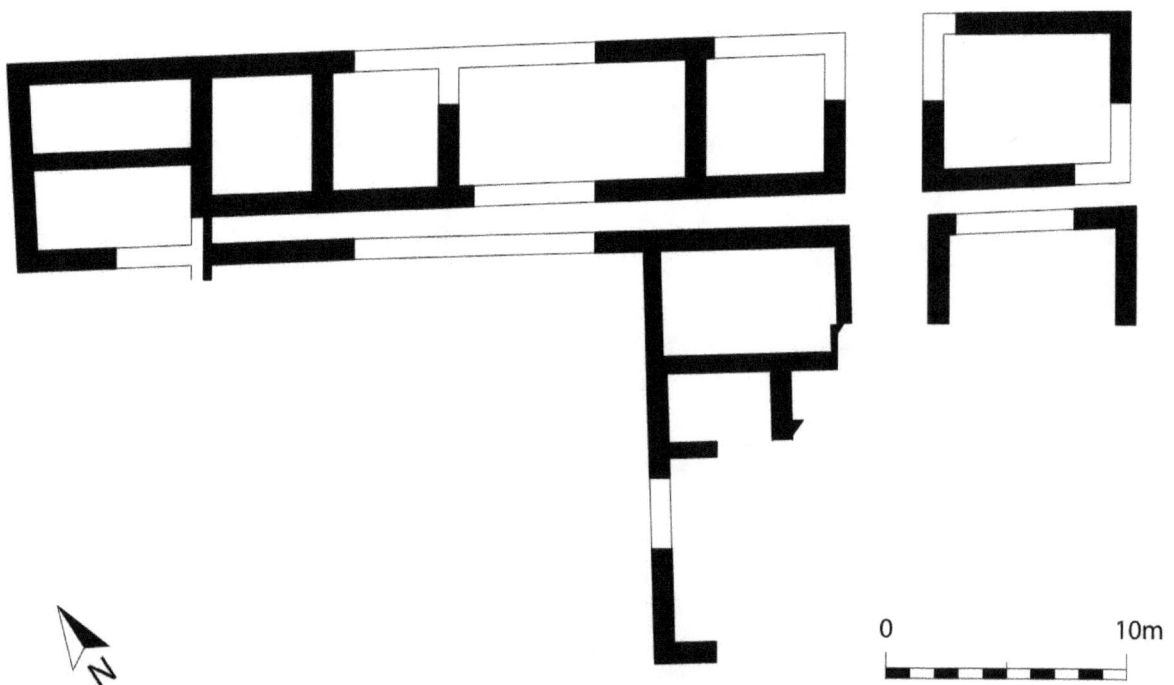

Figure 10. Konopište, foundations of irregular rectangular buildings. (Altered after: P. Popović, 1996)

character and were built of short-lasting material, mostly wood, so their remains were not preserved. It is possible that convoys with food supplies were sent along with military units and builders.

Horreum Margi is mentioned as an important supply and distribution centre of food. Its municipal status indicates its basic function (*CIL* III 7591; *CIL* VI 2388, no. 8).[4] The *Margi* of the title refers to the River Margus, a present-day Morava, on which *Horrea* were situated. Later on, it became the main base for grain distribution to smaller logistic centres along the Danube limes. It kept its basic function as a supply centre for military garrisons in the later period. In the *Notitia Dignitatum, Scutaria Horreomargensis* is mentioned among the four centres of Illyricum under the command of *Magister Officiorum* (*Not. Dign. Or.* XI, 39). Remains of a bridge over the Morava river, mentioned by Kanitz testify to the importance of this area for the Empire (Kanitz 1892, 68-71).

Transportation along limes had to be combined: over both land and river. The supply system over land was well-developed, with a wide network of roads. The problem regarding land transportation was the relatively small weights that could be carried by animals and carts. However, danger along roads could have been caused by robbers (*latrones*) or barbarian intruders during times of war. Therefore every valuable load had to be escorted. The main route was the road along the Danube, connecting all of the limes fortifications, and special importance was given to the road through the Iron Gates constructed under extreme conditions and praised on several imperial tablets (Fig. 11). These tablets celebrate the legions involved in cutting the road through the Iron Gates and later also in its improvement and repair (Šašel 1961, 156-164; Petrović 2004, 71-95). Importance of transport and supply is indicated by the

Figure 11. Roman road cut into the rocks of the Iron Gate gorge. (Doc. of the Institute of Archaeology, Belgrade)

---

[4]   An inscription from 224 AD indicates that the town was a municipium already.

Figure 12. *Tabula Traina*, **image taken from original location. (Doc. of the Institute of Archaeology, Belgrade)**

extreme methods used to enable passage on and along the Danube. The building of the Sip canal, near *Diana* (*Statio Cataractarum Dianae*), under the reign of Trajan was praised as an incredible effort, since only with this canal did the Danube became fully navigable (Fig. 12), since the dangerous cataracts were then able to be avoided (Petrović 1972, 31-39; Jordović 1984, 365-370).

Whenever it was possible, the transport of food and other goods was performed by river. Rivers were used, combined with canals or with a pulling service for upstream navigation. It is assumed that provincial fleets also transported goods for the ground troops (Breeze 2000, 59; Kehne 2007, 328-329). Supplies were delivered along all of the major rivers within the Empire: the Rhine, the Danube, the Nile, the Euphrates etc. Transport along the Danube can be seen on Trajan's column. We can also presume that to the already mentioned great storage building in and other Danube forts, supplies were brought from other parts of the Empire, as well as from the hinterland of the province, mostly along rivers. Actually, the main feature of all of the fortifications along the Danube was river transport. In accordance with this, all of the fortifications had to have a port or some kind of dock, out of which only a few were investigated during the great protective excavations of the Iron Gates limes (Petrović 1991, 207-216).

Possible river ports and stations on the roads, so far, are poorly documented by archaeological data, although there are remains of buildings that could be linked to the fleet and its cells, and are registered in several locations. The most important ports were those next to the legionary camps in *Singidunum* and *Viminacium*, about which there is very little information. Verification of *Singidunum* as a defensive port has not been investigated as, during extensive work by the Serbian Royal Army during 1875, the entire Danube port basin was filled in, a fact which Felix Kanitz also wrote about during his travels around Serbia (Kanitz 1892). The port was probably established at the same time as the fort, forming a united defence system. M. Popović assumed the presence of part of a Danube fleet in *Singidunum*, although there is no evidence of this from written sources (Popović 2006, 39). According to Popović, the position of fortification walls running downhill towards the river bank is similar to defensive systems applied to some of the fortresses of the Iron Gates limes. Such a positioning of ports is known from *Singidunum*, Hajdučka vodenica, *Diana*, *Egeta*. In German literature, such fortified ports are described as Lände-Burgi and they are often encountered along the Rhine limes, although less so along the middle and the lower Danube valley (Höckmann 1986, 369, 399, Abb. 14).

Smaller ports were located in Tekija (*Transdierna*), Čezava (*Novae*), Hajdučka vodenica, Karataš (*Statio Cataractarum Dianae*), Brza Palanka (*Egeta*) and Kusjak near Prahovo (*Aquae*). *Viminacium, Aquae* and *Novae* had ports separated from the main fortification, while at the other sites, the ports were situated next to the fortifications and were protected by perimeter walls which were the main defensive wall of each of the fortifications. As ports of the province of *Moesia Superior*, Margum (*Classis Stradensis et Germensis*), Viminacium (*Prefectus Classis Histricae*), Egeta (*Classis Aegetensium Sive Secunda Pannonica*) and Ratiaria (*Classis Ratiarenses*) are mentioned in (*Not. Dign. Or.* XLII 42, 43).

The fleet *Classis Flavia Moesica* was confirmed first in 92 AD (*CIL* XVI 37), although it most likely existed in the previous decades as well. Some inscriptions testify to the existence of a fleet on the Danube during the period of the 2nd and the 4th centuries AD. The presence of the fleet is confirmed at *Viminacium* in several inscriptions.

Some of the monuments that could be linked to the *collegium nautarum* have been discovered in the vicinity of *Viminacium*. Thus, the port of *Viminacium* is indirectly confirmed by the fragments of marble icons dedicated to Mithras that were raised by a *nauclerus*, the Greek term for latine *navicularius* (Mirković 1986, no. 31).

Deo Invicto M[ithrae – -
nauclerus pos[uit – - -

The existence of Neptune's temple as a feature directly related to the river and river transport was confirmed on several monuments discovered in *Viminacium*. On one of them dedicated to *Matri Deum* a certain *C. Valerius Vibianus, nautarum quinquenalis*, enclosed 2,000 sestertius for the reconstruction of the Temple of Neptune (Mirković, 1986, no. 61).

[Pro salut]e Aug(usti) / C. Val(erius Vi/bianus / nautar(um) q(uin)q(uennalis) sig(num) Ma/tris deum et / ad restitu/tionem tem/pli Neptuni s(estertium) II (milia) n(ummum) d(ono) d(edit).

The existence of a river port at *Viminacium* is still unclear as to whether there were one or two ports whose locations are suggested by remote sensing and field surveys. Unfortunately, only the future excavation of these sites will be able to reveal the exact situation.

It is important to mention a certain *Ulpius Antonius Quintus* who is also known as *aedilis* and *questor* of the *municipium* in *Drobeta*, who decorated the port (*portus*) in Tekija (*Transdierna*) with Juno's sculpture (Vulić 1941-48, no. 469).

Iunoni Regin(a)e
Ulp(ius) Ant(onius) Quintus dec(urio) / aedilic(ius) quaest(or) m(unicipii) D(robetae) ob / honor(em) q(uin)q(uennalitatis) port[u]s

In conclusion, we could say that the complex system of the supply and distribution of goods in the territory of the province of *Moesia Superior*, was conducted via land and river throughout the Roman period. Unfortunately, possible river ports and stations are, archaeologically, very poorly documented. Apart from greater supply centres, in which food supplies were stored and kept for further distribution

(Porečka reka, *Horreum Margi*), according to the archaeological data preserved, forts along the Danube limes also had their own buildings intended for storing food for the soldiers stationed within them for a certain period of time. The supply system used by the Roman army, and the method of collecting supplies within the larger supply centres, indicate that the quantity of grain produced in the province of the *Moesia Superior* was not sufficient for all of the inhabitants and soldiers stationed in its territory. This shortfall was covered with imports from the neighbouring provinces, such as the areas around the Black Sea and *Dacia*, but also from distant parts of the Roman Empire.

7

Conclusion

By studying the contents of the material culture of rural settlements and agricultural estates of the *villa rustica* type and also dealing with problems of supplying, storing and the transportation of agricultural products it is possible to draw conclusions which will contribute to a better understanding of the establishment and development of agriculture in the Roman provinces of the Central Balkans (south-eastern *Pannonia Inferior* and *Moesia Superior*, later *Pannonia Secunda, Moesia Prima, Dacia Ripensis* and *Dacia Mediterranea*), as well as allowing a better comprehension of the changes brought about by the process of urbanisation from the 1st to the first half of the 5th century. Taking into account the material remains and considering the geophysical and climatic characteristics of the area, the regional differences, the local traditions and social and cultural aspects, it is clear that the material which we had at our disposal during investigations is still not sufficiently comprehensive to allow us to draw general or more definite conclusions. However, on the basis of available archaeological data and preserved historical written sources, we have partially identified the conditions that determined the scope of economic activity during the period of Roman domination and, as segment of that, agriculture as a fundamental activity in those areas.

The territory of Vojvodina and central parts of Serbia make up a segment of a wider geographic region, which we could denote as the middle and lower Danube basin and the Central Balkans region. This region was, for many centuries in the past, connected via the rivers Danube and Sava with Central Europe and Italy in the west and with eastern areas of the Balkans as far as the Black Sea in the east, while it was in permanent contact with the Mediterranean world via the valleys of the Velika Morava and Vardar. Regarding its economic importance, it could easily be stated that it was a very important region in Europe as a result of the characteristics of its geographic position, its relief and climate, the structure of the soil, its hydrographic characteristics and its flora and fauna. Its favourable position, natural resources, especially the fertile soil in Pannonia and the river valleys, and its considerable mineral wealth made the region attractive for the Roman Empire in a strategic as well as an economic sense. The natural and climatic conditions of the territory were favourable for developing agricultural production in the plains where farming was practiced on large, regularly parcelled out estates typical of Pannonia and the valleys of large rivers such as the areas around *Viminacium*, the Velika Morava valley and in the area around *Naissus*, while the hilly and mountainous regions were suitable for stockbreeding. Besides those favourable geophysical characteristics and the natural resources of the Balkan region, the entire way of life of the population was influenced by new organisation of their economic activities, including agricultural production, introduced by the Romans in the process of establishing their administration in the region and also by other socio-economic factors.

Particularly important, not only from a military point of view but also for economic progress, was the construction of the road along the right bank of the Danube River. Roman emperors also used this for their campaigns in the East because it was well protected by the system of military fortifications built along the Danube. Its economic significance considerably increased after Trajan's conquest of the provinces across the Danube in AD 107, as this secured for a long period of time peace and undisturbed economic development on the Danube as well as commercial traffic with other parts of the Empire.

When considering the territory of the Central Balkans, it stood out during the entire antique period as an agrarian and insufficiently urbanised region. A few areas could be distinguished for their intensive agriculture, which was certainly the result of favourable natural factors: relief, soil structure, hydrological and climatic characteristics. Primarily this was the area of the Pannonia province, that is, the territory of present-day Srem and Mačva. The valleys of the big rivers were also important agricultural regions, with the most important being the Velika Morava valley. According to the archaeological investigations carried out so far in that region we can see that the entire territory of Srem and Mačva was an intensively agricultural region. Soil cultivation and the agricultural tools used on the estates organised as *villae rusticae* were certainly more technically advanced than those used in the pre-Roman period. Particularly densely populated was the region toward the Sava River, which can be explained as a consequence of the proximity to the main communication and because of the gravitation toward *Sirmium* as the centre of the wider region. If we examine the disposition of villas within the investigated territory we can see that they were mostly built along rivers, with areas to the left and right of the river banks left open for cultivation. Buildings in the plains were usually constructed on elevated ground. In the hilly regions such structures were built on river terraces at the end of slopes, mostly oriented in a north-south direction and with their entrance to the south.

Another important factor that determined the location of villas was certainly their proximity to the communication routes, which made possible the distribution of products from the estate. There is no doubt that the direction of certain roads had an impact on the construction of villas, making it possible to connect with urban centres, to which they supplied agricultural products.

Their proximity to village settlements also had impact on the location of the villas as such settlements could provide a labour force if necessary for seasonal work on the estate. This is confirmed at the villas at the sites of Dumbovo, near Beočin and Kudoš, near Šašinci etc.

It is concluded on the basis of hitherto conducted archaeological investigations of Roman rural settlements (*vici*) and agricultural estates (*villae rusticae*) that architectural complexes of villas were mostly constructed at the locations of previously created, early imperial settlements from the 1st and 2nd centuries, or in their immediate vicinity. Such a situation has been confirmed within the territory of the Pannonia province (Dumbovo, near Beočin, Šašinci and Hrtkovci), where topographic investigations and partial archaeological excavations of *vici* and *villae rusticae* have made possible the comprehension of the changes bought about during the process of urbanisation. Most of the autochthonous settlements were included in the new plan of urbanisation that the Romans started to put into effect in the 1st century AD. Their existence can be traced until the Flavian dynasty, at the latest. On the other hand, it has been established, based on the topographic data of the recorded sites, that Roman settlements were organised in the vicinity of important communications, at locations providing favourable conditions for the exploitation of natural resources and the labour force from the nearby autochthonous settlements. Until the establishment of *villae rusticae*, those settlements, which were the result of the urbanised deduction system, represented significant economic units for supplying larger urban centres. The *vicus* at Dumbovo, organised on the slopes of Fruška Gora in the frontier zone of the limes, is a good example of a Roman rural settlement established by veterans' deduction, as suggested by the inscription on a border stone. The inscription mentions the allotment of the land of the village of Iosista, *vicus Iosista*, to Titus Claudius Priscus praefectus of *ala I civium Romanorum*, in the second half of the 1st century.

Inhabitants of the *vici* took part in the economic activities of the nearest agricultural estates, which were already established by the end of the 1st century and unified with them from an economic perspective. Most of these estates were constructed along the major road connection *Sirmium* and *Singidunum*. It is most probable that the labour force on those estates was chiefly drawn from the village population, members of the autochthonous population. Production on the estates was initially on a smaller scale, generally to satisfy only their own needs, but later, as a result of organisational changes in the method of soil cultivation, the *villae rusticae* took on an increasingly important role in the economic life of the province. Besides agriculture, they were also engaged in other economic activities, mostly practicing various crafts and developing commercial networks for selling their products, inevitably resulting in social and economic divisions in the population and an increase in the speed of Romanisation. During the 2nd and 3rd centuries, the number of villas with an urbanised area and land for agricultural activities and the development of certain craft activities increased at the locations of former autochthonous settlements, or *vici*.

Villae rusticae as complex production units possessed everything required for the functioning of an independent economy: residential building, various economic structures, workshops for manufacturing and repairing tools, and land for cultivation. The urbanistic concept of a villa depended on the industries which prevailed in the area, but also on the type of ownership of the estate, whether it was an estate of a large landowner or the emperor or just the estate of a small owner such as a free peasant. It is assumed that villas within the wider city territory of *Sirmium* were imperial estates. Regarding their architectural concept and decorative contents these villas were certainly residential in character. However, they also included land for agricultural activities and artisans' workshops.

A distinct type of property is an *ager adsignatus*, which is related to the deduction of veterans when, by the process of assigning, the property of veterans was exempted from the *peregrine civitates*. Similar to the situation in other Danube provinces, veterans in the region of the limes located in the provinces of Lower Pannonia and Upper Moesia belonged, in the 2nd and 3rd centuries, to the class of medium landowners, and their land was worked by tenant farmers or slaves. Such a situation is indirectly indicated by dedications to agrarian deities on the inscriptions of veterans. This is evident in one such inscription on a votive *ara* discovered within the wider territory of *Singidunum* and dedicated to the cult of Liber and Libera (Dušanić, Mirković 1976, no 16, 52-53).

A large economic crisis in the Empire at the end of the 3rd century and reforms carried out by Diocletian as a consequence of the crisis, imposed the need, in the 4th century, to reorganise and restore the villas, which were incorporated in the economic system of the Empire as important units. In the second half of the 4th century, at a time of increasing insecurity on the frontiers, villas took on a fortified character with the construction of towers and their adaptation to structures for house guards who protected inhabitants and food. Such adaptations are noticeable on some structures, for instance the basilical building in the villa at Šašinci that had the function of a *horreum*, or the adaptation of the apse in the tower in the later phase of the villa at the site of Livade, in the vicinity of Sremska Mitrovica. At the same time, villas were fortified with the construction of watch-towers (*speculae*), such as those recorded in Dumbovo and Šašinci.

In the time of Valentinian I and in the post-Valentinian period, the foederati settled in the vicinity of Roman villas. This is confirmed by the material remains recorded at a few sites in Vojvodina (the remains of small hamlets consisting of a few huts and open hearths were recorded at the sites in Krnješevci and Kuzmin). A period of the general disintegration of Roman-provincial culture ensued, which would eventually completely disappear with the arrival of new ethnic elements. They brought a new system of economy and new forms of agricultural production, thus marking the end of Late Roman period and the beginning of the Great Migration at the end of 6th and the beginning of the 7th century.

The large number of monetary hoards, mostly dating from the second half of the 4th century, speaks about the tempestuous events that characterised the Late Roman period in the Pannonian-Balkan region. A particularly large quantity of hoards was discovered in Mačva, with most of them dated from the second half of the 4th century. The fact that this region was not spared from destruction is even more clearly demonstrated in the remains of *villae rusticae*. In many structures it has been recorded that life stopped violently, as suggested by the layer of conflagration at most of the investigated sites. It is probable that at some locations the estates were restored but, as systematic excavations have not been conducted at most of the sites, we cannot yet expect a reliable answer to this question.

Since the time of Diocletian and, later, Constantine the Great, changes in the military organisation took place with the introduction of standing frontier troops, *milites limitanei*, who, according to established scientific opinion, were village militia consisting of soldier-peasants. The earliest sources, which suggest that the *limitanei* worked land obtained from the state, date from the year 443. Taking into account certain finds discovered within some Late Roman fortifications, we can reasonably assume the existance of civil settlements in the vicinity of the Late Roman fortifications on the limes in the second half of the 4th and the beginning of the 5th century. Whether these were settlements for the families of the *limitanei* or civil settlements of a rural type, established near the camps in order to supply frontier garrisons, we cannot answer with any certainty at this time.

The system of supplying and storing provisions for the army and the population and the system of storing reserves at large collection points indicates that the production of grain and other staple foods in the Upper Moesia region was not sufficient for feeding either the army stationed in its territory or the population. This shortage was compensated for by importing from neighbouring provinces, primarily from the regions around the Black Sea, but we should also consider imports from other, even farther, parts of the Empire.

It is conspicuous that supplying the army with provisions was very advanced in the Late Roman period and that the procurement and distribution of food were organised by military commanders who were also in charge of supply. They had at their disposal the *horrea* outside military camps that were collection points from which food was distributed. One such important structure was built at the confluence of the Porečka and Danube rivers.

In addition to the large collection points in which supplies of food were stored and preserved for further distribution, fortifications on the limes also had their own structures intended for storing provisions that could satisfy the needs of the army units stationed there for a specific period of time. Evidence of this includes the preserved remains of a few military granaries in fortifications on the Danube Limes.

The method of delivering food must have involved a combination of both land and river transportation. The main supply system for the fortifications on the Danube about which we have most data so far was river transportation. Consequently, the fortifications must have had piers, but only few of them have been archaeologically confirmed.

The least known element in the system of Roman agriculture is the size of the estates, which consequently raises the question of property relationships. It is still insufficiently defined whether there were smaller estates of free peasants or large estates which were allotted to the coloni to work, as most of the investigated villas in the territory of Serbia are from the 4ᵗʰ century.

Here, yet another problem appears that awaits a final resolution, the question of the direct labour force on the estates and, related to that, the position of the autochthonous population. In that context, it should be noted that the role of free tenant farmers is still not precisely determined and that we draw all conclusions on the basis of assumptions. It should be borne in mind that the Roman state, from the time of the great economic and political disturbances of the 3ʳᵈ century, started to bind free peasants to land and this intensified particularly during the 4ᵗʰ century when they became *coloni originals*. This process of tying peasants to land was certainly also practiced in the Balkan provinces of the Empire. Tenant farmers probably worked the land of the municipal aristocracy or that of veteran estates but, over the course of time, their number decreased, primarily because of their more frequent engagement in military service, and slave labour became more frequently used. This fact is confirmed by the preserved epigraphic data from the 3ʳᵈ century where it is stated that in addition to land, soldiers were also given slaves and livestock.

A final answer also awaits the question concerning the structure and scope of property relationships. Available historical sources and material remains still do not offer a definitive answer to the question of who the owner of certain lands was and who was working on it, what the relationship was between *ager publicus* and the territory of certain legions (*territorium legionis*), a problem also encountered in other provinces of the Empire. Nevertheless, we should also emphasise that the results of more recent investigations where original sources, regardless of their scarcity, still make it possible to comprehend to a certain extent the increase of large land estates in the 4ᵗʰ century, although the borders between imperial estates and municipal territories are still imprecisely defined. Despite many questions remaining unanswered, we can assume, on the basis of preserved material remains and written documents that the area of the Central Balkans provinces was important as a region of large land estates and that imperial domains had an important place among them.

After examining all the gathered evidence regarding production units in agriculture; the new agricultural estates of the *villa rustica* type, the structures for storing, and the transportation and distribution of agricultural products, we arrived at the conclusion that the population of the Central Balkans in the Roman period was mostly engaged in agriculture. Agriculture could be carried out on the large, regularly parcelled estates that were characteristic of the area of Pannonia and the valleys of larger rivers, such as the area of *Viminacium*, the Velika Morava valleys and the areas around *Naissus*. Organisational changes in the methods of tilling and the cultivation of land, together with the application of new technologically more sophisticated tools and new methods of animal husbandry inevitably had an impact on the economic and social division of the population and the process of Romanisation. It was more intensive in the plains compared to the hilly and mountainous areas where, because of the less favourable natural conditions and the isolation of the areas, traditional forms of economy were generally preserved throughout the entire Roman period.

8

Catalogue of Excavated Roman Rural Settlement Sites

The following catalogue includes all the Roman rural settlement sites (*vici, villae rusticae*) used in the study.

Vici

The southeastern part of the province of *Pannonia Inferior* (Vojvodina)

Dumbovo, Beočin

A Roman *vicus* at Dumbovo, near Beočin was identified on the slopes of Fruška Gora in the border zone of the limes in the Roman province of Pannonia. The chance find of a border stone with an inscription mentioning *vicus Iosista* suggests an early Romanisation of this area. M. Mirković offered a more detailed interpretation of the inscription and, in her opinion, the settlement was established by the process of veteran deduction in the second half of the 1st century AD. The inscription on the stone speaks about assigning land of the *Iosista* village to *Titus Claudius Priscus*, the prefect of the *ala – ala I civium Romanorum-* in the second half of the 1st century AD (Mirković 1971, 81-82, no 79, pl. XII/1).

In the settlement, in pit houses of an elliptical shape and with rectangular open hearths, fragments of *terra sigillata*, imported Italic glass and fibulas have also been found, along with local pottery characterised by coarse handmade pots. On the other hand, ceramic spindle whorls and flint tools indicate an autochthonous economic system was still in existence. Using the typological and stratigraphic analysis of dwelling structures and archaeological material, the settlement ceased to exist in the first years of the 2nd century. This was the time of the reorganisation of the frontier defensive system and when the auxiliary troops would have been deployed on the Danube banks. Archaeological investigations have revealed that after the abandonment of the pit houses, i.e., the disappearance of that type of settlement, a rather small country estate – a *villa rustica* with specula – was established in the valley, later in the 4th century.

References: Brukner, Olga. "Rimsko naselje kod Beočina." *Materijali* XIII, (1977): 123-136; Brukner, Olga. "*Vicus* i *villa rustica* u pograničnoj zoni limesa između Cusum-a i Bononia-e." *Građa za proučavanje spmenika kulture Vojvodine* VI-VII, (1976): 19-43; Mirković, Miroslava. *Sirmium. Its History from the I Century A.D. to 582 A. D. Sirmium* I, Beograd: Arheološki institut, 1971.

Vranj, Hrtkovci

A similar process of the establishment of a *villa rustica* in the location of an early Roman *vicus*, as in the previously mentioned site at Dumbovo, is also characteristic of the multi-layered site at Hrtkovci, with the foundations of the villa dug into the remains of a structure from the early Roman period.

Below the wall foundation at the south side a cultural pit was identified. It was filled with animal bones and numerous fragments of Roman-provincial pottery and glass characteristic of the 1st to 2nd century. Besides the large amount of local vessel shapes, there were many fragments of *terra sigillata* imported from northern Italian workshops, fragments of beakers, small bowls, plates, censers, lids and the base of an amphora. Particularly important is the fragment of an amphora rim with the stamp of the potter, *Calvia Crispinilla*, executed in ligature. This was a product imported from a workshop in Istria. During the early imperial period the workshop produced and transported its products along the Sava valley as far as Pannonia.

Many years of investigations on both sides of the site of Vranj in Hrtkovci revealed over twenty pottery kilns with pits for the preparation and discarding of material. They indicate well-developed local artisan production in this area during the 1st and 2nd centuries that emerged thanks to favourable local conditions: good quality clay and the proximity of a navigable waterway, which made possible the transportation of goods eastward and westward (Brukner 1992, 53-70).

References: Dautova-Ruševljan, Velika. "Vranj, Hrtkovci – antički lokalitet." *AP* 24, (1985): 110-114; Dautova-Ruševljan, Velika. "Zaštitna iskopavanja rimskog naselja u Hrtkovcima 1991 godine." *RVM* 35, (1993): 53-70; Dautova-Ruševljan, Velika. "Sistematsko zaštitna iskopavanja u Hrtkovcima." *Glasnik SAD* 15-16, (1999-2000): 163-168; Brukner, Olga. "Novi nalazi imitacije tere sigilate panonske radionice «X» *Zbornik NM* XIV." (1992): 373-378.

Rural settlements along the route of the modern highway through Srem

During the rescue archaeological excavations along the route of the modern highway through Srem, performed between 1973 and 1987, Roman *vici* and *pagi* have also been discovered beside the settlements of the native population. These settlements were related to the newly-established municipal territories of *Sirmium* and *Basianae* and to the main road between *Sirmium* and *Singidunum*. According to preserved archaeological finds, their inhabitants were natives. In all the settlements investigated so far, the type of dwellings and economy reveals a strong prehistoric tradition along with the remains of a Roman material culture. Finds of pottery vessels and other objects used in everyday life have revealed the rural character of these settlements. On the other hand, however, in the pottery material from the newly-established settlements, it can be seen that, besides local products, there is also a considerable amount of Italic import, including *terra sigillata* and other Romanised forms.

With the establishment of smaller Roman estates at the end of the 1st century AD, inhabitants from these hamlets were included in the economic activities of the nearest estates, thus forming an economic unity with them. It has also been revealed that early Roman settlements from the 1st and 2nd centuries in Srem were usually situated in an area where later architectural and building complexes of the *villa rustica* type were built, or in their immediate vicinity.

Thus, at the site of Kudoš in the village of Šašinci, there are stratigraphically distinguished remains of a Roman *vicus* from the Flavian period, situated in an area where a *villa rustica* was later built. In the early imperial settlement, huts were identified of a semi-subterranean type and rubbish pits where Italic import, early imperial provincial ceramics and products of autochthonous pottery have been discovered. A similar situation has also been recorded at sites in Krnješevci, Prhovo and Kuzmin.

References: Brukner, Olga. "Rimska naselja i vile rustike." *Arheološka istraživanja duž autoputa kroz Srem,* edited by Vapa Zoran, 137-174. Novi Sad: Pokrajinski zavod za zaštitu spomenika kulture 1995.

The province of *Moesia Superior* (central Serbia)

Bube, Belgrade

The settlement, in the vicinity of *Singidunum* is the only so far investigated *vicus* in the territory of the Upper Moesia province. This *vicus Bube* is mentioned on one Roman altar dedicated to Hercules. There is no other information about the settlement. The title of *princeps praefectus* for a local leader had probably already been abandoned by the end of the 1st century. The names of the dedicants in the inscription are Latin with the imperial gentile names of *Flavius* and *Aelius*, indicating that their ancestors were granted Roman citizenship under the emperors of the 1st and 2nd centuries, hence the inscription, could be dated to the end of the 2nd century (Mirković 99-102). The location of the *vicus Bube* in the immediate vicinity of antique *Singidunum* confirms the assumption that *vici* were established near larger urban centres in order to supply them with agricultural products.

References: Mirković, Miroslava. "Rimsko selo Bube kod Singidunuma." *Starinar* XXXIX, (1988): 99-104.

Table 1. Excavated Roman *vici* in the territory of Serbia (Central Balkan)

Site	Location	Province	Century
Dumbovo, Beočin, Srem	Roman limes. Later, the villa was built on the site near the *vicus*	*Pannonia Inferior*	1st-2nd century
Kudoš, Šašinci; Srem	Main road between *Sirmium* and *Singidunum*. Later, the villa was built on the site near the *vicus*	*Pannonia Inferior*	1st-2nd century
Malo Kuvalovo, Krnješevci; Srem	Main road between *Sirmium* and *Singidunum*	*Pannonia Inferior*	1st century
Vranj, Hrtkovci, Srem	Left bank of the Sava River. Later, the villa was built on the site near the *vicus*	*Pannonia Inferior*	1st-2nd century
Bube, near Belgrade	Vicinity of *Singidunum*	*Moesia Superior*	1st-2nd century

Villae rusticae

The southeastern part of the province of *Pannonia Inferior* or *Pannonia Secunda* (present-day Vojvodina)

Dumbovo, Beočin (later habitation horizon)

The villa was built in the frontier zone of the Pannonian limes in the sector between the castrum *Cusum* (Petrovaradin) and the castrum *Bononia* (Banoštor).

It is a villa with a watch-tower (*specula*). The architectural complex consists of three investigated structures. Structure 1 corresponds to the type of Pannonian villa with a central corridor (Fig. 13). The second structure (2), which was, by all appearances, connected to structure 3, has been significantly damaged by stream erosion. The structure was built on top of the remains of a hut from the 1st century AD. It was most probably an economic structure with a courtyard surrounded by porches for storing animal fodder, grain, tools, etc. To the west of structure 2, the northern section of the third structure, building 3, was discovered.

Figure 13. Beočin, Dumbovo. Site plan – *vicus* and *villa rustica*. (Altered after: O. Brukner, 1976)

A *specula* with a square ground plan that was erected at an elevation served as protection for the inhabitants and to prevent enemies passing through the valley into the interior of the province.

Many finds, various types of tools including an axe, a shovel, a hammer, a chisel, a rasp and iron slag were discovered within the area of all three structures.

Time of construction and habitation: The villa was built in the 4th century. Finds of Roman provincial pottery characteristic of the 4th century, fibulas and coins of emperors from the 4th century (35 bronze coins), minted in Rome, *Siscia, Sirmium*, Thessalonica, Antioch have been discovered at the site. The coins discovered were issued by the following Emperors: Constantine the Great, Licinius, Constantius II, Valens, Valentinianus I and Gratianus.

Two building phases are apparent at the site: the 1st and 2nd centuries with remains of huts and a later phase with remains of the 4th century villa.

References: Brukner, Olga. "Rimsko naselje kod Beočina." *Materijali* XIII, (1977): 123-136; Brukner, Olga. "*Vicus* i *villa rustica* u pograničnoj zoni limesa između Cusum-a i Bononia-e." *Građa za proučavanje spmenika kulture Vojvodine* VI-VII, (1976): 19-43.

Surroundings of Sirmium

Remains of many villas, a watch-tower (*specula*) and necropolises, as well as an octagonal structure have been discovered at the locations denoted as Livade and Mitrovačke Livade, to the northeast of Sremska Mitrovica. The topographic ubication of the villas indicates a well organised urbanisation around the city of *Sirmium* in areas suitable for agriculture and where good communications and approaches to the city existed. Considering their size, architectural design and decorative content, they were certainly of a residential character but, at the same time, they had land for agricultural activities and also artisans' workshops. The distance between the recorded villas was 800-1000 m. It is important to mention that such a distance between villas is not characteristic for other regions of Srem.

The site of Livade, Sremska Mitrovica

The villa is situated in the immediate vicinity of Sremska Mitrovica, near a necropolis. Part of the central building within the villa complex with a few rooms linked by a corridor and with an entrance strengthened with corner pilasters has been investigated.

Time of construction and habitation: The findings were dated to the 3rd to the 5th centuries.

References: Brukner, Olga. "Rimska naselja i vile rustike. "*Arheološka istraživanja duž autoputa kroz Srem,* edited by Vapa Zoran, 137-174. Novi Sad: Pokrajinski zavod za zaštitu spomenika kulture 1995.

The site of Livade Mitrovačke, Sremska Mitrovica

The villa complex was partially discovered in the immediate vicinity of a Roman rural settlement from the 1st-2nd century. A *specula* was situated within the complex. It was built in the immediate vicinity of a building with preserved foundations of stone rubble joined with mortar. Considering the proximity of Sirmium's northern city wall it is most probable that its function was not just the protection of the villa but also of the city itself.

Time of construction and habitation: Pottery material indicates that this complex was in use in the 3rd to the 5th centuries.

References: Brukner, Olga. "Rimska naselja i vile rustike. "*Arheološka istraživanja duž autoputa kroz Srem,* edited by Vapa Zoran, 137-174. Novi Sad: Pokrajinski zavod za zaštitu spomenika kulture 1995.

Kudoš, Šašinci

The site of Kudoš is situated in the vicinity of the village of Šašinci, in Srem. The villa is located around 1.5 km from the important *Sirmium-Singidunum* road. The villa complex consisted of a basilical building with an apse and a few smaller economic structures. A *specula* was also within the villa complex (Fig. 14).

Time of construction and habitation: Archaeological material and coins suggest two phases of habitation, a settlement of a rural type from the time of the Flavians (*vicus*) and a *villa rustica* from the 3rd and 4th centuries. The cultural layer within the wider zone of the villa contains objects of diverse purpose, some of which were produced in local workshops, such as relief decorated bowls imitating *terra sigillata* ware. Other archaeological material includes fragments of glass vessels, bracelet of glass

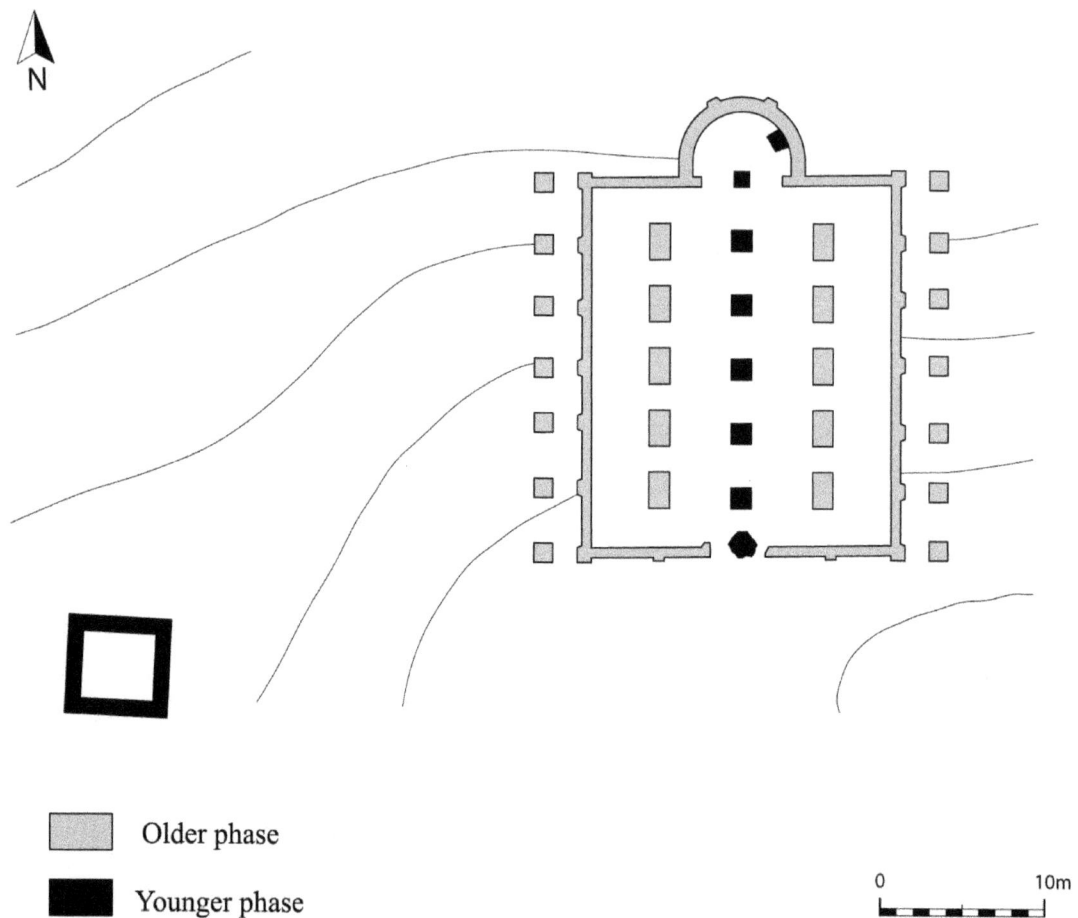

Older phase

Younger phase

0   10m

Figure 14. Kudoš, Šašinci. Bsilical structure and tower in the complex of the villa. (Altered after: O. Brukner, 1995)

paste, bone pins and needles, iron knives, chisel, a trilobate tanged arrowhead and wedges. A find of a monetary hoard and individual coin pieces dates the villa to the 3rd and 4th centuries.

References: Brukner, Olga. "Kudoš, Šašinci – villa rustica." *AP* 21, (1980): 108-109; Brukner, Olga. "Kudoš, Šašinci – villa rustica." *AP* 23, (1982): 93-95; Brukner, Olga. " Kudoš, Šašinci – villa rustica." *AP* 24, (1985): 99; Brukner, Olga. "Rimska naselja i vile rustike. "*Arheološka istraživanja duž autoputa kroz Srem,* edited by Vapa Zoran, 137-174. Novi Sad: Pokrajinski zavod za zaštitu spomenika kulture 1995.

Vranj, Hrtkovci

The remains of five more villas were recorded in the area of the village of Hrtkovci, in Srem which, besides the *villa rustica* at the site Vranj, are so far the most thoroughly investigated. The five villas were discovered at the sites of: Starčevo Brdo, Jarčina (two villas), Vukoder and Simote. The building complex of the villa covers an area of around one hectare. Some rooms of the villa have been partially investigated (Fig. 15). The walls were built of brick and stone joined with lime mortar. Remains of a brick built hypocaust indicate that there was floor and vertical heating in the villa. A rather large quantity of fresco fragments was found in one of the rooms of the villa. The motifs of the frescoes comprised vegetal and geometric ornaments, realised in various nuances and shades (Fig. 16).

Time of construction and habitation: Noteworthy discovered material used in everyday life by the villa inhabitants includes pots, lids, bowls, needles, spindle whorls, lamps, hairpins, fibulas, iron

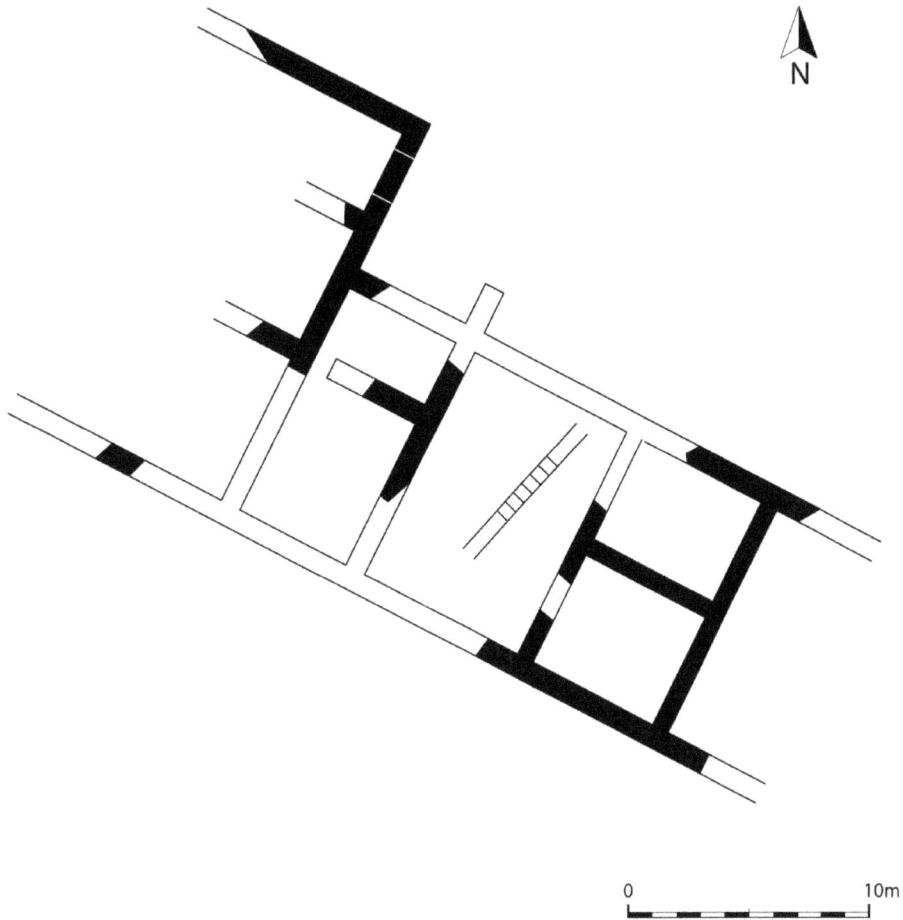

Figure 15. Hrtkovci. Plan of partially investigated walls of the villa. (Altered after: V. Dautova Ruševljan, 2005)

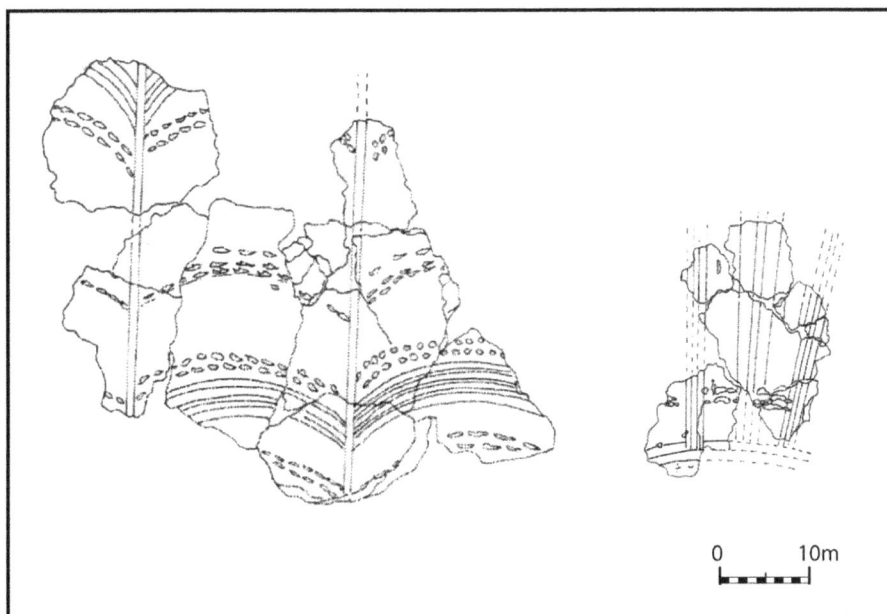

Figure 16. Hrtkovci, Fresco remains in the villa. (Altered after: V. Dautova Ruševljan, 2005)

wedges and clamps. Besides these finds, coins of Gallienus, Constantius II and Constans have also been discovered, indicating continuous habitation on the estate within the wider city zone of *Sirmium* from the mid 3rd to the mid 4th century.

References: Dautova-Ruševljan, Velika. "Vranj, Hrtkovci – antički lokalitet." *AP* 24, (1985): 110-114; Dautova-Ruševljan, Velika. "Zaštitna iskopavanja rimskog naselja u Hrtkovcima 1991 godine." *RVM* 35, (1993): 53-70; Dautova-Ruševljan, Velika. "Vila rustica na lokalitetu Vranj u Hrtkovcima." *RMV* 41-42, (1999-2000): 15-28; Dautova-Ruševljan, Velika. "Sistematsko zaštitna iskopavanja u Hrtkovcima." *Glasnik SAD* 15-16, (1999-2000): 163-168; Dautova-Ruševljan, Velika. "DautovaVila rustika u Hrtkovicima, sistematsko zaštitna iskopavanja." *Zbornik Matice srpske za klasične studije* 6, (2004): 171-173; Dautova-Ruševljan, Velika. "Sistematsko-zaštitna iskopavanja vile rustike u Hrtkovcima 2004. godine." *Glasnik SAD* 21, (2005): 239-249; Dautova-Ruševljan, Velika and Brukner, Olga. *Gomolava, rimski period*, Novi Sad: Muzej Vojvodine, 1992.

The province of *Moesia Superior* or *Moesia Prima* (present-day central Serbia)

Štitar, Mačva

A *villa rustica* of rectangular shape consisting of three rooms, one of which has an apse at one end has been encountered at this site. There is a pentagonal room projecting out of the villa facade from the north-eastern corner. According to E. Thomas, the building should be identified as the villa type with projecting towers at the corners (Eckrisalit), which is known to have existed in Pannonia in the 4th century (Thomas 1964, 359, Abb. 174). The building's foundations were made of stone rubble and brick joined with lime mortar. Two of the villa's rooms had open hearths.

Time of construction and habitation: In addition to the fragments of pottery showing characteristics of *Sirmium* pottery from the middle and second half of the 4th century, coins of Licinius minted in *Siscia* have also been encountered. A number of burials were discovered somewhat further from this building, with certain of the grave goods also being dated to the 4th century.

References: Vasić, Miloje. "Mačva i Podrinje u rimsko doba." *Glasnik SAD* 2, (1985): 124-141.

Anine, Lajkovac

In the village of Ćelije near Lajkovac, at the site of Anine, in the vicinity of the Kolubara River, the remains of an antique site were discovered with the partially preserved remains of a Roman *villa rustica*, one of the larger such discoveries in western Serbia (Fig. 17). The building complex covers an area of around 4,000 square meters, of which around 2,000 square meters were used for storing agricultural products. The remains of six rooms with walls preserved up to a height of 2 meters have been discovered thus far. The villa had a system for under floor heating, indicated by the remains of a hypocaust in the central room with the apse. The walls were built in the *opus incertum* technique using broken and half-dressed stone and additional bricks set in mortar. The floors in all three rooms were made of high quality lime mortar. Despite the fact that the discovered structures are partially explored, we think that this was a relatively big complex of a Late Roman villa with structures constructed at the beginning of the 4th century and destroyed in a conflagration at the end of the 4th century, judging by the coins discovered on the floor of the room with the apse.

Time of construction and habitation: The large quantity of finds indicates that the villa was in intensive use in the 4th century. Although the discovered structures are only partially explored, it seems that this was a large complex of a Late Roman villa with structures built at the beginning of the 4th century that were destroyed in a conflagration at the end of the 4th century, during the Gothic invasions of the Balkans. This is suggested by the coins found on the floor of the room with the apse.

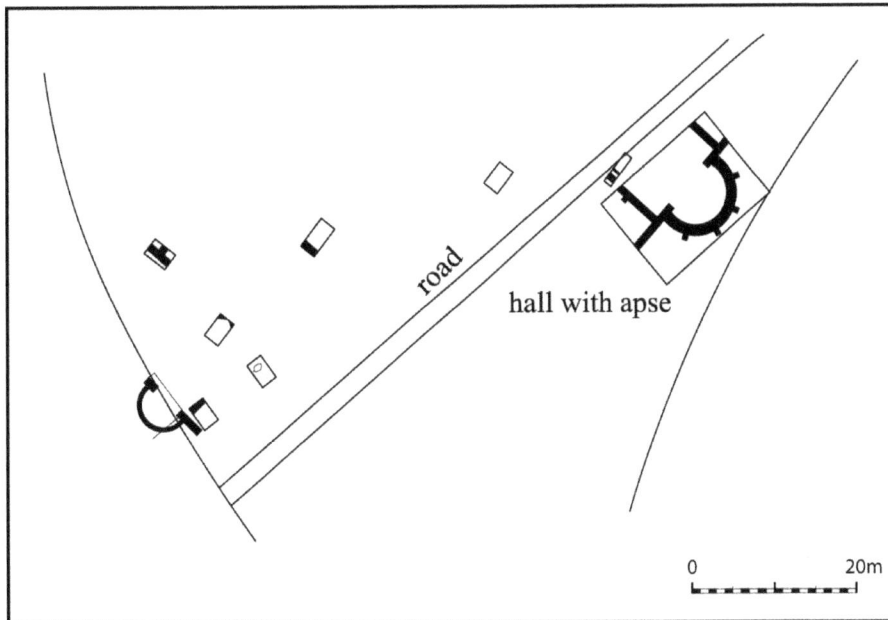

Figure 17. Anine, Lajkovac, Site plan of the *villa rustica* complex. (Altered after: R. Arsić 2009)

Somewhat further to the north of the described structures a large amount of archaeological material including fragments of fibulas, bracelets of glass paste, finger rings as well as coins from the period between the 2nd and 4th century was discovered. These finds indicate the existence of a necropolis in that area. Such an assumption is supported by the discovery of a fragment of a funerary stela. Finds of coins from the 2nd century suggest the possibility of the existence of an earlier rural settlement of the *vicus* type in the vicinity of the villa complex. It would appear that sometime later an agricultural estate of the *villa rustica* type was established and, thus, had been maintained in continuity with the earlier settlement. This is a situation that has been confirmed for most of villas investigated so far in Srem, as well as in the larger area of the Pannonia province, as has already been mentioned earlier.

References: Arsić, Radivoje "Istraživanja poznoantičkog lokaliteta Anine u selu Ćelije opština Lajkovac." *Glasnik DKS* 31, (2007): 56-60; Arsić, Radivoje "Istraživanje kasnoantičke vile na lokalitetu „Anine" 2008. godine." *Glasnik DKS* 33, (2009): 88-90.

Viminacium – Livade kod Ćuprije

At the site of Livade, near Ćuprija, situated 650 meters to the southwest of *Viminacium*, a *villa rustica* of a rectangular ground plan that consists of eight rooms and one large corridor in the central area was discovered. The villa was built of stone, brick and mortar using techniques frequently applied in building similar structures. It belongs to the type of villa with a rectangular ground plan and with a central corridor. Three more villas besides this one were recorded in the vicinity of *Viminacium*, at the sites of Na Kamenju, Stig and Burdelj (Fig. 2).

Time of construction and habitation: Archaeological finds discovered in the villa rooms (pottery, glazed lamp) indicate the 4th century as the time of construction and use of the villa.

References: Jovivičić, Mladen and Redžić, Saša. "Late Roman villa on the site Livade kod Ćuprije: a contribution to the study of villae rusticae in the vicinity of Viminacium." *Archaeology and Science* 7, (2012): 369-385.

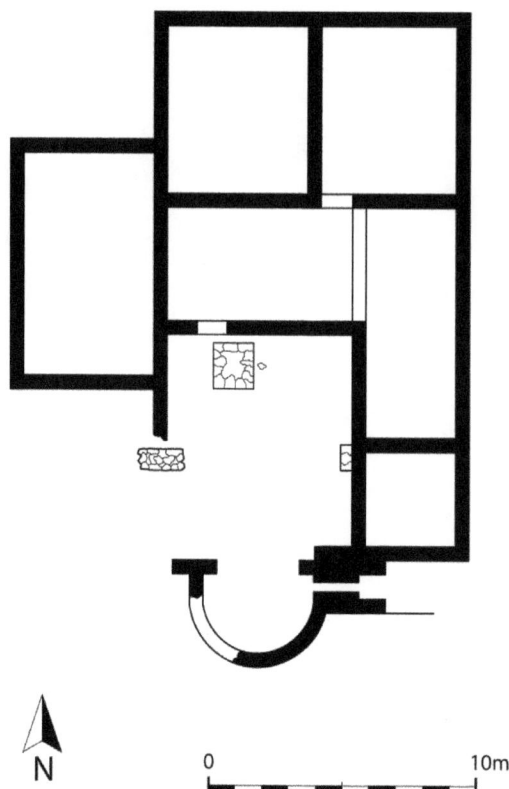

Figure 18. Poskurice, Kragujevac. Plan of partially explored structure in the villa complex. (Altered after: D. Petrović, 1966)

Poskurice, Kragujevac

At the site Poskurice, the building is partially investigated and situated at the southern end of the structure was a room with an apse at one end (Fig. 18). The foundations were built of stone rubble joined with lime mortar. Traces of purple and grey paint are visible on some fragments of the mortar.

At the eastern external side of the building, next to the apse, was a vaulted furnace connected to canals going through the rooms of the building, identified as the remains of the villa's hypocaust system.

Time of construction and habitation: Roman bronze coins were found, most of them poorly preserved or damaged. The coins discovered were issued by the 3rd century Emperors Valerian and Gallienus.

References: Petrović, Dragoljub. "Ostaci rimske građevine u Poskuricama." *Starinar* XV-XVI, (1966): 253-256.

Višesava, Bajina Bašta

The building at the site of Višesava, near Bajina Bašta consists of a few rooms of uneven size, with two of them ending in semicircular apses (Fig. 19). The walls were built of half-dressed stone and the foundations are relatively shallow. The structure consisting of one fairly large central room with a semicircular apse at one end, a series of smaller rooms, a long entrance area to the west and a likely portico was a building within the complex of a Roman villa.

Time of construction and habitation: The difficulty of making a more precise chronological determination of the structure is due to the fact that only a very small amount of archaeological material

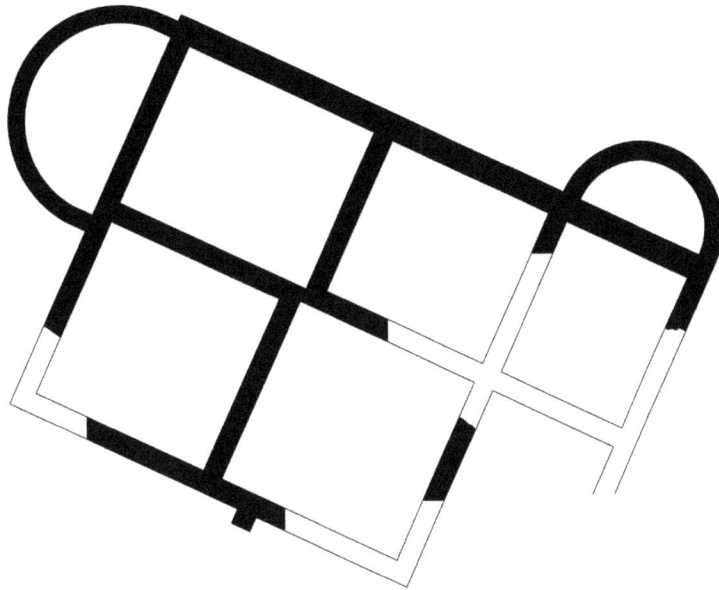

Figure 19. Višesava, Bajina Bašta. Plan of partially explored structure in the villa complex. (Altered after: J. Bućić, P. Petrović, 1986)

was discovered inside the structure. Only a few fragments of pottery vessels (pots and bowls, of brown colour and coarse fabric) were found which were, based on their appearance, locally produced. Bearing in mind the analogies with villas from Pannonia, it is assumed that this villa was also built in the 2ⁿᵈ to 3ʳᵈ century, when villas with porticos still did not have towers as there was no need for additional protection of agricultural estates.

References: Bućić, Javorka and Petrović, Petar. "Rimske ciglarske peći i vila u Bakionici kod Požege." *Užički zbornik* 13. (1984) 5-22; Bućić, Javorka and Petrović, Petar. "Rimska vila u Višesavi kod Bajine Bašte" *Užički zbornik* 15, (1986): 23-42.

Gornja Gorevnica, Čačak

An architectural complex consisting of a few structures was encountered at the site of Dublje, in the village Gornja Gorevnica, around 10 km to the north of Čačak. A building, with a large entrance (around 4 meters), was on the southern side of the complex. The lower sections were built of stone rubble and river pebbles joined with lime mortar. The floor was made of lime mortar mixed with gravel, topped with a layer of mortar. For the upper sections of the structure, timber framing was used. The roof covering consisted of tegulae and imbreces. This structure had an economic purpose within the complex of the *villa rustica*. Yet another building with an apse has only been partially explored. The area covered by the entire agglomeration could have been approximately 100 x 80 meters and could be classified into the category of smaller agricultural estates. The structure was destroyed in a conflagration at the end of the 4ᵗʰ century.

Time of construction and habitation: The discovered of archaeological material includes two whetstones, a rather small knife blade, a fragmented glass beaker which dates from the second half of the 4ᵗʰ century and a bronze coin of Valentinian I, minted in 364.

References: Vasić, Miloje. "Kasnoantička nalazišta u Čačku i okolini." In *Bogorodica Gradačka u istoriji srpskog naroda*, Naučni skup povodom 800 godina Bogorodice Gradačke i grada Čačka 1992, edited by Milovan Vulović, 9-17. Čačak: Narodni muzej 1993.

Prijevor, Čačak

The building complex is on the left bank of the Zapadna Morava river, in the vicinity of the town of Čačak. The investigated structures include a residential building, a granary and another, somewhat small, economic structure. The residential building is oriented in an east-west direction, of rectangular shape and has five rooms. The eastern section consists of three rooms, with the central one ending in an apse. The southern room had a hypocaust system for heating. The building foundations were made of large pebbles joined with mud, while the upper section of the building was timber-framed, as with the previously mentioned structure. Similarly, the floors of this building were also coated with mortar.

Discovered to the west of this building were foundations of a structure opened to the north with a floor paved with cobblestones, while the roof structure consisted of tegulae and imbreces. The remains of a granary were discovered around 100 meters to the southeast of this structure.

Time of construction and habitation: The precise date of construction of the villa could not be established, but the date of its destruction is more certain. Within the residential building a fragment of a glass beaker was discovered which, according to its decoration, could be dated from the second half of the 4th century to the beginning of the 5th century. Recovered pottery fragments also correspond to a production date of the 4th century.

One memorial with two burials was discovered and partially investigated at the neighbouring site of Čuljevina. Despite the fact that they had been plundered, a portion of the grave inventory is preserved and it is characteristic of the end of 4th and the first half of the 5th century. The owners of the villa were, according to the investigators of the site, most probably buried in the graves. As a consequence of this assumption, the construction of the memorial could be considered the *terminus post quem* for the abandonment of the villa.

References: Vasić, Miloje. "Kasnoantička nalazišta u Čačku i okolini." In *Bogorodica Gradačka u istoriji srpskog naroda*, Naučni skup povodom 800 godina Bogorodice Gradačke i grada Čačka 1992, edited by Milovan Vulović, 9-17. Čačak: Narodni muzej 1993.

Beljina, Čačak

The structure situated to the southwest of the Roman baths, which belonged to a Roman agricultural estate, a villa was partially investigated at the site of Jakovina, near Čačak, on the right bank of the Zapadna Morava river. The complex covered an area of around 100 x 70 m and it represents a rather small agricultural estate.

Time of construction and habitation: Two phases of habitation have been identified. The first phase dates, according to the discovered pottery material, from the mid 2nd to the mid 3rd century. Following this earliest phase, the pottery material indicates a continuity of living in this area from the end of 4th to the first decades of the 5th century.

References: References: Vasić, Miloje. "Kasnoantička nalazišta u Čačku i okolini." In *Bogorodica Gradačka u istoriji srpskog naroda*, Naučni skup povodom 800 godina Bogorodice Gradačke i grada Čačka 1992, edited by Milovan Vulović, 9-17. Čačak: Narodni muzej 1993; Cvjetićanin, Tanja. "Rimska keramika iz Čačka i okoline." *ZRNMČ* XVIII, (1988): 103-119.

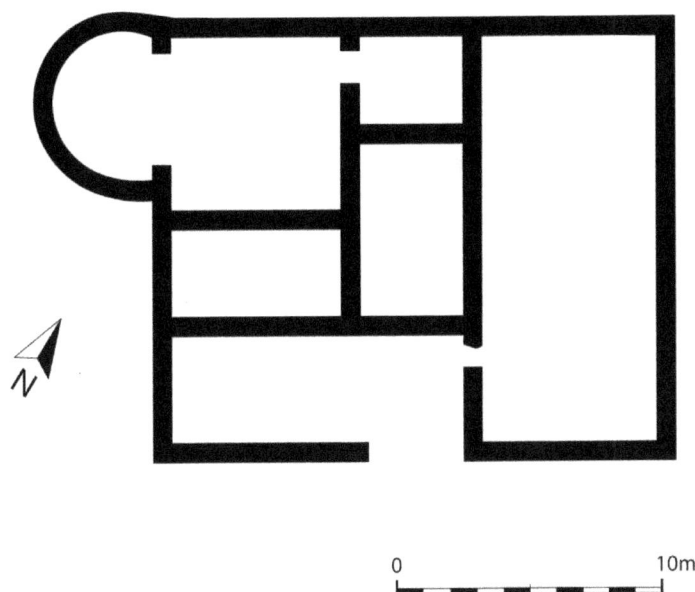

Figure 20. Krivelj, Bor. Plan of building in the villa complex. (Altered after: M. Jevtić, 1996)

Krivelj, Bor

The building, of a rectangular ground plan, consists of six unequally sized rooms (Fig. 20). According to the arrangement of the rooms, this building could be typologically identified as a villa with a corridor. Such a villa type is well represented in *Pannonia*, as well as more to the south, in *Moesia Superior* and is characteristic of a Late Roman form of the *villa rustica*.

Time of construction and habitation: The discovered of finds include a bronze figure of the goddess Venus, a cruciform fibula, fragments of glazed pottery, a few fragments of pottery lamps, etc. Particularly interesting for the dating of the building is a bronze bracelet with finely engraved stylised representations of snakes' heads, which appear in the provinces of Upper Moesia and Pannonia in Late Antiquity, from the end of the 3rd to the first half of the 5th century. The discovery of bronze coins (16 pieces) from the earliest specimens of Aurelian to the latest from the time of Theodosius also chronologically determine the use of the building from the end of 3rd to the end of 4th century.

References: Jevtić, Miloš. "Keramika starijeg i mlađeg gvozdenog doba sa nalazišta Staro Groblje u Krivelju kod Bora." *Zbornik NM* XVI/1, (1996): 129-142; Jovanović, Aeksandar. *Nakit u rimskoj Dardaniji*, Beograd: Savez arheoloških društava Jugoslavije, 1978.

Gamzigrad, Zaječar

In the south-eastern section of the imperial palace complex, a structure was discovered and partially explored (only the narrow northern side was explored, dim. 11.5 x 10.5 m), with two longitudinal rooms and a portico in the east (Fig. 21). The walls of the building were made of brick and stone in the *opus mixtum* technique.

Time of construction and habitation: The building was demolished in the course of the construction of the structures of the palace complex, at the beginning of the 4th century. Bronze coins minted in the time of the emperors Aurelian and Probus were discovered in a layer of soot on top of the corridor's mortar floor and they mark the *terminus post quem* for the construction of the building. The building was

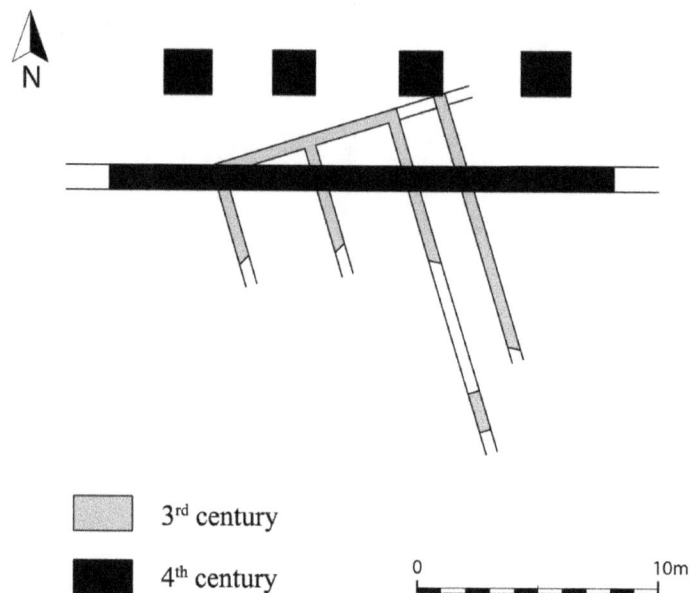

Figure 21. Gamzigrad, Zaječar. Plan of the villa in the area of the large temple. (Altered after: S. Petković, 2011)

certainly in use before that time, as suggested by objects discovered in its vicinity, within Gamzigrad's ramparts and in the area to the south of them, which included: fragments of pottery vessels, pottery lamps, and bronze fibulas dating from the 2nd and 3rd centuries. Together, all the mentioned finds indicate that this *villa rustica* might have been built in the first half of the 3rd century.

References: Srejović, Dragoslav. "Rimsko poljsko imanje." In *Gamzigrad, kasnoantički carski dvorac*, edited by Stojan Ćelić, 21-23. Beograd: Galerija SANU 1983; Petković, Sofija. "Rimski Gamzigrad pre carske palate." In *Felix Romuliana – Gamzigrad*, edited by Ivana Popović, 33-42. Beograd: Areološki institut 2010; Petković, Sofija. "The Roman Settlement on Gamzigrad prior to the Imperial Palace Felix Romuliana." *Starinar* LXI, (2011): 171-190.

Kržince, Vladičin Han

The site of Sveti Trojica in the village of Kržince, near Vladičin Han is situated high in the hills on one of the terraces descending to the village stream. The villa complex consists of two segments, the northern one of which comprises two unequal rooms of an approximately square ground plan. The southern part of the structure is almost identical in shape and size to the northern (Fig. 22). A passage between the rooms is linked in the west with a portico, of which only traces remain. The walls were built in a dry-wall technique of broken stone joined with mud. The wall facing was made of partially dressed stone blocks.

Time of construction and habitation: According to the archaeological finds, the building could be dated to the second half of the 4th century. Discovered pottery vessels include: pots, bowls, plates, lids and pithoi. The forms of the pottery represent typical kitchen ware characteristic of the 4th century. Besides the coarse ware of local manufacture, some pottery vessels of fine fabric were most probably imported from the neighbouring provinces where workshops for the production of grey *terra sigillata* already existed.

In addition, two ceramic weights of a pyramid shape have been discovered at the site of Sveti Trojica. Fragments of glass vessels were found in abundance and those for which it has been possible to identify

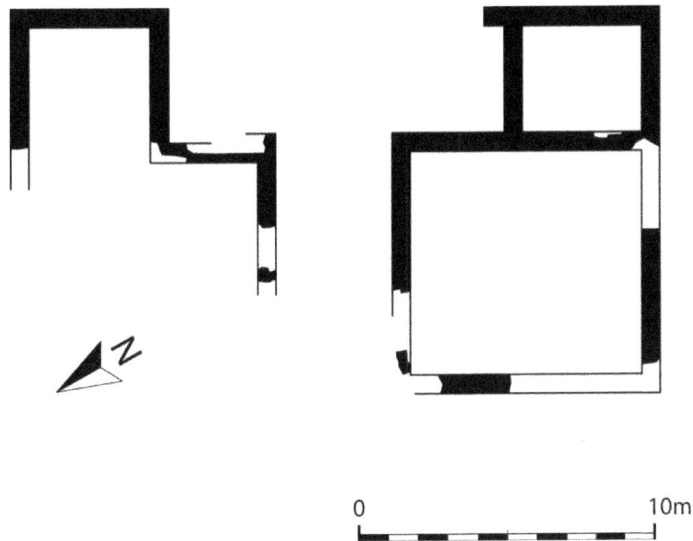

Figure 22. Kržince, Vladičin Han. Plan of partially explored structure in the villa complex. (Altered after: M. Ružić, 2005)

typologically are mostly beakers which, according to their features, are characteristic of the Late Antique period.

Objects of iron mostly include wedges and clamps from the wooden parts of the building. Also, an iron escutcheon and key most probably originate from the entrance door. Two iron tools indicate the possible function of the discovered structure. These are an iron punch and a crescent shaped leather scraper.

The absence of a distinct layer of destruction indicates that the building was abandoned abruptly, most probably before the attacks by barbarians, possibly Goths, that were frequent in the Central Balkans at the end of the 4th century.

References: Ružić, Mira. "Kržince – Sveti Trojica, kasnoantička vila." In *Arheološka istraživanja E-75*, edited by Marin Brmbolić, 205-225. Beograd: Republički zavod za zaštitu spomenika kulture 2005.

Table 2. Excavated villas in the territory of Serbia (Central Balkan)

Site	Type	Province	Century
Dumbovo, Beočin	Pannonian villa with a central corridor; There is a specula	(Panonnia Secunda)	4th century
Livade, Sr. Mitrovica	Pannonian villa with a central corridor	Pannonia Inferior (Panonnia Secunda)	3rd-4th century
Mitrovačke Livade, Sr. Mitrovica	The villa complex was partially discovered. It was built in the vicinity of a Roman rural settlement from the 1st-2nd century. Later a specula was built	Pannonia Inferior (Panonnia Secunda)	3rd-4th century
Kudoš, Šašinci	The villa complex consisted of a basilical building with an apse and a few smaller economic structures. A specula was also within the villa complex	Pannonia Inferior (Panonnia Secunda)	3rd-4th century
Vranj, Hrtkovci	Some rooms of the villa have been partially investigated. The villa complex was built in the vicinity of a Roman rural settlement from the 1st-2nd century	Pannonia Inferior (Panonnia Secunda)	3rd-4th century
Štitar in Mačva	Villa with projecting towers at the corners (Echrisalit)	Moesia Prima	4th century
Anine, Lajkovac	Some rooms of the villa have been partially explored (six rooms). It is one of the larger discovered villa in Serbia. The villa complex was built in the vicinity of a Roman rural settlement from the 1st-2nd century	Moesia Prima	4th century
Viminacium – Livade near Ćuprija	Pannonian villa with a rectangular ground plan and central corridor	Moesia Prima	4th century
Poskurice, Kragujevac	The villa complex is partially investigated. At the southern end of the structure there was a room with an apse	Moesia Superior	3rd century
Višesava, Bajina Bašta	Villa with porticos ?	Dalmatia	2nd-3rd century
Gornja Gorevnica, Čačak	A building with an apse has only been partially explored ?	Moesia Prima	4th century
Prijevor, Čačak	The residential building is of rectangular shape and has five rooms. The villa complex is partially investigated	Moesia Prima	4th-5th century
Beljina, Čačak	Some rooms of the villa have been partially explored. It is a rather small agricultural estate.	Moesia Superior Moesia Prima	First phase: 2nd-3rd century; second phase: end of 4th to ½ 5th century
Krivelj, Bor	Pannonian villa with a corridor	Dacia Ripensis	The end of 3rd to the end of 4th century
Gamzigrad, Zaječar	In the south-eastern section of the imperial palace complex, a villa was discovered and partially explored with two longitudinal rooms and a portico in the east	Dacia Ripensis	3rd century
Kržince, Vladičin Han	A complex of villa has only been partially explored. A passage between the rooms is linked in with a portico	Dacia Mediterranea	4th century

List of Sites with Possible Roman Villas

Archaeological excavations and surveys carried out on the territory of Vojvodina and central Serbia in recent decades have allowed the registration of a significant number of sites belonging to the Roman period. Their character can be deduced more than it can be precisely defined, but most of them are constructions of housing complexes, where it is not always possible to draw a clear distinction between a settlement type, a *vicus*, and an agricultural estate type, a *villa rustica*. Their identification can only be made indirectly based on the remains of architecture (tegulae, imbreces and traces of walls).

The southeastern part of the province of *Pannonia Inferior* (*Pannonia Secunda*) (present-day Vojvodina):

- Čortanovci na Fruškoj Gori
- Ilinci
- Mala Remeta
- Veliki Radinci
- Bregovi-Atovac, Kuzmin
- Međaš, Kuzmin
- Zlatara Ruma
- Kudoške livade, Ruma
- Voganj
- Klenak
- Gajići, Adaševci
- Prosine, Pećinci
- Prosine, Prhovo
- Deč
- Karlovčić
- Donji Tovarnik
- Ašanja
- Mačvanska Mitrovica
- Salaš Noćajski
- Noćaj
- Zasavica

The central part of the province of *Moesia Superior* (*Moesia Prima*) (present-day central Serbia):

- Bela Reka, Šabac
- Mrđenovac, Šabac
- Miokus, Šabac
- Nakučani, Šabac
- Drenovac, Šabac
- Metković, Bogatić
- Mačvanski Pričinović, Šabac

- Ševarice, Šabac
- Ravnje, Mačvanska Mitrovica
- Debrc, Vladimirac
- Vlasenica, Vladimirac
- Donje Crniljevo, Koceljeva
- Sokolova, Lazarevac
- Stepojevac, Lazarevac
- Kolubarski Leskovac
- Bakionica, Požega
- Vinik, Niš
- Gorica, Niš
- Bojnik-Direktorovo, Leskovac
- Vrbovac-Imanje Pešića, Leskovac
- Podrimce-Belije, Leskovac
- Ograđe, Leskovac

Ancient Sources

Amm. Marc. – *Ammianus Marcellinus*, *Roman History* (English trans. by John C. Rolfe), vol I-III. London – Cambridge Mass. 1963-1964.

Aur. Vict. *De caes.* – *De Caesaribus*, Epitome incerti, (ed.) Franz Pichlmayer, Leipzig 1911.

Cato, Varro, *De agricult.* – Cato and Varro, *On Agriculture* (Cato, Varro, *De agricultura*), (English trans. by W. D. Hooper, H. B. Ash), London-Cambridge Mass. 1967.

Cod. Theod. – *Codex Theodosianus*

Digest. – *Corpus iuris civilis* vol. I, *Institutiones, Digesta*, edited by P. Krüger, T. Mommsen, Berolini 1889

Dio Cass. – Dio Cassius, *Roman History* (Dio. Cass. *Historia Romana*), (English trans. by E. Cary), London-Cambridge- Mass. 1969.

Eutrop. – Eutropius, *Breviarum ab urbe condita*, (ed.) F. Ruehl, Leipzig: Teubner 1887.

Lib. *Or.* – Libanius, *Selected Orations*, (English trans. by A. F. Norman), The Loeb Classical library, London – Cambridge Mass. 1977.

Not. Dign. Or. – *Notitia Dignitatum*, ed. O. Seeck, Berolini 1876.

Plin., *Nat. Hist.* – Pliny, *Natural History* (Plinius, *Naturalis historia*), (English trans. by H. Rackham), The Loeb Classical library, London – Cambridge Mass 1967.

Priskos – *Vizantijski izvori za istoriju naroda Jugoslavije* I, edited by Georgije Ostrogorski Beograd: SAN Posebna izdanja, 1955.

Tac. *Agr.* – Tacitus, *Agricola*, (English trans. by M. Hutton), London – Cambridge Mass. 1970.

Tac. *Ann.; Tac. Hist.* – Tacitus, *The Annals of Tacitus* (books I-III), *The Histories of Tacitus*, (books IV-V), (English trans. by J. Jackson), London – Cambridge Mass. 1969.

Theoph. Sym. – *Vizantijski izvori za istoriju naroda Jugoslavije* I, edited by Georgije Ostrogorski Beograd: SAN Posebna izdanja, 1955.

Vitruv. *De architect.* – Vitruvius, *Ten Books on Architecture*, (English trans. by M. Hicky Morgan), London – Cambridge Mass. 1960.

Bibliography

A

Arsić, Radivoje. "Istraživanja poznoantičkog lokaliteta Anine u selu Ćelije opština Lajkovac." *Glasnik DKS* 31 (2007): 56-60.

Arsić, Radivoje. "Istraživanje kasnoantičke vile na lokalitetu „Anine" 2008. godine." *Glasnik DKS* 33 (2009): 88-90.

B

Begović, Vlasta and Schrunk, Ivančica. "Maritime Villas on the Eastern Adriatic Coast, (Roman Histria and Dalmatia)." In *The Roman Empire and Beyond: Archaeological and Historical Research on the Romans and Native Cultures in Central Europe,* edited by Eric De Sena and Halina Dobrzanska, 3-22. Oxford: British Arhcaeological Reports 2011.

Biró, M. "Roman villas in Pannonia." *Acta Arch.* XXVI fasc.1-2 (1974): 23-57.

Blažić, Svetlana. "Ostaci životinjskih vrsta sa lokaliteta na trasi auto-puta kroz Srem." In *Arheološka istraživanja duž autoputa kroz Srem,* edited by Vapa Zoran, 331-346. Novi Sad: Pokrajinski zavod za zaštitu spomenika kulture1995.

Bošković, Đurđe, Duval, Noël and Popović, Vladislav. "Jugoslovensko-francuska istraživanja Sirmijuma 1973. godine." *Starinar* XXIV-XXV: 193-200.

Bratanić, Rudolf. "Arheološka istraživanja u Brzom Brodu." *Starinar* XIII (1938): 199-204.

Breeze, J. David. "Supplying the Army." In: *Kaiser, Heer und Gesellschaft in der Römischen Kaiserzert: Gedenkschriftfür Eric Birley*, edited by Géza Alföldy, Brian Dobson and Werner Eck, 59-64. Stuttgart: Franz Steiner Verlag, 2000.

Brukner, Olga. "Rimsko naselje kod Beočina." In *Antički gradovi i naselja u Južnoj Panoniji i graničnim područjima. Materijali* XIII, edited by Branka Vikić-Belančić, 123-136. Beograd: Antička sekcija SADJ, Hrvatsko arheološko društvo, Gradski muzej u Varaždinu, 1977.

Brukner, Olga. "*Vicus* i *villa rustica* u pograničnoj zoni limesa između Cusum-a i Bononia-e." *Građa za proučavanje spmenika kulture Vojvodine* VI-VII (1976): 19-43.

Brukner, Olga. *Rimska keramika u jugoslovenskom delu provincije Donje Panonije,* Dissertationes et monographie. Beograd: Pokrajinski zavod za zaštitu spomenika kulture, Savez arheoloških društava Jugoslavije,1981.

Brukner, Olga. "Kudoš, Šašinci – villa rustica." *AP* 21 (1980): 108-109.

Brukner, Olga. "Prosine, Prhovo – rimsko naselje." *AP* 21 (1981): 108-109.

Brukner, Olga. "Kudoš, Šašinci – villa rustica." *AP* 23 (1982): 93-95.

Brukner, Olga. " Kudoš, Šašinci – villa rustica." *AP* 24 (1985): 99.

Brukner, Olga. "Novi nalazi imitacije tere sigilate panonske radionice «X» *Zbornik NM* XIV." (1992): 373-378.

Brukner, Olga. "Domorodačka naselja." In *Arheološka istraživanja duž autoputa kroz Srem,* edited by Vapa Zoran, 91-136. Novi Sad: Pokrajinski zavod za zaštitu spomenika kulture1995.

Brukner, Olga. "Rimska naselja i vile rustike." In *Arheološka istraživanja duž autoputa kroz Srem,* edited by Vapa Zoran, 137-174. Novi Sad: Pokrajinski zavod za zaštitu spomenika kulture1995.

Brukner, Olga, Dautova-Ruševljan, Velika and Milošević, Petar. *Počeci romanizacije u jutositočnom delu provincije Panonije.* Novi Sad: Matica Srpska,1987.

C

Carrié, Jean Michel. "Diocletien et la fiscalité." *Antiquité tardive* 2 (1994): 33-64.

Cavallo, Chiara, Koistra, I. Laura and Dütting, K. Monica. "Food supply to the Roman army in the Rhine delta in the first century A.D." In *Feeding the Roman army. The archaeology of production and supply in NW Europe,* edited by *Sue Stallibrass and Richard Thomas,* 69-82. Oxford: Oxbow Books, 2008.

Cvijić, Jovan. *Balkansko poluostrvo i južnoslovenske zemlje* I. Beograd: Državna štamparija, 1922.

Cvjetićanin, Tanja. "Rimska keramika iz Čačka i okoline." *ZRNMČ* XVIII, (1988): 103-119.

Č

Čerškov, Emil. *Rimljani na Kosovu i Metohiji,* Beograd: Arheološko društvo Jugoslavije, 1969.

Čerškov, Toni. "Mediana-horreum." *AP* 25 (1986): 41-43.

D

Dautova-Ruševljan, Velika. "Rimski novac sa arheoloških iskopavanja na lok. Dumbovo kod Beočina." Građa za proučavanje spomenika kulture Vojvodine VI-VII (1976): 45-47.

Dautova-Ruševljan, Velika. "Vranj, Hrtkovci – antički lokalitet." AP 24 (1985): 110-114.

Dautova-Ruševljan, Velika. "Sondažno-zaštitno iskopavanje rimske nekropole u Hrtkovcima." RVM 34 (1992): 91-105.

Dautova-Ruševljan, Velika. "Zaštitna iskopavanja rimskog naselja u Hrtkovcima 1991 godine." RVM 35, (1993): 53-70.

Dautova-Ruševljan, Velika. "Vila rustica na lokalitetu Vranj u Hrtkovcima." RMV 41-42 (1999-2000): 15-28.

Dautova-Ruševljan, Velika. "Sistematsko zaštitna iskopavanja u Hrtkovcima." Glasnik SAD 15-16 (1999-2000): 163-168.

Dautova-Ruševljan, Velika. "Vila rustika u Hrtkovicima, sistematsko zaštitna iskopavanja." Zbornik Matice srpske za klasične studije 6 (2004): 171-173.

Dautova-Ruševljan, Velika. "Sistematsko-zaštitna iskopavanja vile rustike u Hrtkovcima 2004. godine." *Glasnik SAD* 21 (2005): 239-249.

Dautova-Ruševljan, Velika and Brukner, Olga. *Gomolava, rimski period,* Novi Sad: Muzej Vojvodine, 1992.

Davies, W. Roy. *Service in the Roman Army.* Edinburgh: Edinburgh University Press, 1989.

De Sena, Eric. "An assessment of wine and oil production in Rome's hinterland: ceramic, literarty art historical and modern evidence." In *Roman villas around the Urbs, Interaction with landscape and Enviroment*, edited by Klynne A. and Santilli Frizell, B., 1-15. (www.svenska-institutet-rom.org).

Dimitrijević, Danica. "Sapaja, rimsko i srednjovekovno utvrđenje na ostrvu kod Stare Palanke." *Starinar* XXXIII-XXXIV, (1984): 29-71.

Drča, Slobodan. "Medijana – objekat B" *Zbornik* 9 (2000): 21-31.

Dušanić, Slobodan. "Bassianae and its territory." *Arch. Iug.* VIII (1967): 67-81.

Dušanić, Slobodan. "Rimska vojska u istočnom Sremu." *Zbornik FF* X/1 (1968): 87-113.

Dušanić, Slobodan. "Epigrafske beleške, *civitas Sirmiensium et Amantinorum.*" *ŽA* XXVII (1977): 179-192.

Dušanić, Slobodan and Mirković, Miroslava. *Singidunum et le nord-ouest de la province. IMS*, vol. I, Beograd: *Centre d'études épigraphiques et numismatiques* de la Faculté de philosophie de l'Université de Beograd, 1976.

Dušanić, Slobodan. "The legions and the fiscal estates in Moesia Superior: some epigraphical notes." *AV* 41 (1990): 585-596.

Duval, Noël and Popović, Vladislav. *Horrea et thermae aux abords du rempart sud.* Sirmium 7, Collection de L'école francaise de Rome 29/1. Rome-Belgrade: L'école francaise de Rome, Institut archèologique de *Belgrade*, 1977.

Đ

Đokić, Danica and Jacanović, Dragan. "Topografska građa Stiga." *Viminacium* 7 (1992): 61-110.

F

Ferjančić, Snežana. "The Prefecture of Illyricum in the 4th Century." Mélanges d'histoire et d'épigraphie (1997): 231-239.

Ferjančić, Snežana. Naseljavanje legijskih veterana u balkanskim provincijama I-III vek n.e. Beograd: Balkanološki institut SANU, 2002.

Ferri, Naser. "Nekoliko epigrafskih svjedočanstava o providbi i štovanju božanstava voda u Gornjoj Meziji." Histria Antiqua 21 (2012): 307-313.

Filipović, Mil. "Arheologija i etnologija." Leskovački zbornik 8 (1968): 5-8.

Finley, I. *Moses.* The Ancient Economy. Berkeley: University of California Press, 1999.

Fitz, Jeno. "Economic life," In The Archaeology of Roman Pannonia, edited by A. Lengyel, and G. T. B. Radan, 323-335. Budapest: The University Press of Kentucky, Akadémiai Kiadó, 1980.

G

Gabričević, Martin. "Rtkovo-Glamija I: Une forteresse de la basse epoque." Cahiers des Portes de Fer III (1986): 71-91.

Garašanin, Milutin and Garašanin, Draga. *Arheološka nalazišta u Srbiji.* Beograd: Prosveta, 1951.

Garašanin, Milutin, Vasić, Milolje and Marjanović-Vujović, Gordana. "Trajanovi most – castrum Pontes." Cahiers des Portes de Fer II (1984): 25-84.

Grenier, Albert. Manuel d'archéologie gallo-romaine 2, L'archéologie du sol. Paris: Editions A. Picard, 1934.

Green, Kevin. *The Archaeology of the Roman Economy*. Berkeley and Los Angeles: University of California Press, 1990.

H

Höckmann, Olaf. "Römische Schiffsverbönde auf dem Ober und Mittelrhein und die Verteidigung der Rheingrenze in der spätantike." *Jahrbuch des römisch-germanischen Zentralmuseums Mainz* 33 (1986): 369-416.

I

Isaak, Benjamin. "The Meaning of the Terms *Limes* and *Limitanei*." *JRS* LXXVIII (1988) 125-147.

J

Jeremić, Gordana. *Saldvm: Roman and Early Byzantine Fortification*. Belgrade: Institute of Archaeology, 2009.

Jeremić, Miroslav. "Sirmijum u periodu tetrarhije." In *Rimski carski gradovi i palate u Srbiji*, edited by Dragoslav Srejović, 89-114. Beograd: Galerija SANU, 1993.

Jevtić, Miloš. "Keramika starijeg i mlađeg gvozdenog doba sa nalazišta Staro Groblje u Krivelju kod Bora." *Zbornik NM* XVI/1 (1996): 129-142.

Jocić, Mira. "Arheološko nalazište u Bojnku. "*Leskovački zbornik* XXIX (1989): 289-295.

Jones, Arnold Hugh Martin. The Later Roman Empire (AD 284-602): a social, economic and administrative survey, Vol. I-II, Oxford: Basil Blackwell, 1973.

Jordović Časlav. "Ostaci rimskog puta u Djerdapskoj klisuri." *Starinar* XXXIII-XXXIV (1984): 365-370.

Jovičić, Mladen and Redžić, Saša. "Late Roman villa on the site Livade kod Ćuprije: a contribution to the study of villae rusticae in the vicinity of Viminacium." *Archaeology and Science* 7, (2012): 369-385.

Jovanović, Aleksandar. *Nakit u rimskoj Dardaniji*, Beograd: Savez arheoloških društava Jugoslavije, 1978.

Jović, Đorđe. Sirmium, lokalitet 30, *AP* 4, Beograd 1962, 144-150.

K

Kanitz, Felix. *Römische Studien in Serbien. Der Donau-Grenzwall, das Strassennetz, die Städte, Castelle, Denkmale,Thermen und Bergwerke zur Römerzeit im Königreiche Serben.* Wien: Tempsky 1892.

Kehne, Peter. "War – and Peacetime Logistics: Supplying Imperial Armies in East and West." In: *A Companion to the Roman Army*, edited by Paul Erdkamp, 323-338. Malden-Oxford-Carlton: Blackwell Publishing, 2007.

Kilić-Matić, Ana. "Prilog proučavanju tehnika i struktura gradnje rimskih vila rustika na obali rimske provincije Dalmacije." *Opuscula Archaeologica* vol. 28/1 (2004): 91-109.

Kostić, S. Đorđe. *Dunavski limes Feliksa Kanica*. Beograd: Arheološki institut, 2011.

Krunić, Slavica. "Upotrebni predmeti (Utilitarian Objects)." In *Antička bronza Singidunuma (Antique bronze from Singidnunum)*." edited by Slavica Krunić, 189-207. Beograd: Muzej Grada Beograda 1997.

Kuzmanović-Cvetković, Julka. *Prokuplje, grad Svetog Prokopija*, Prokuplje: Muzej Toplice, 1998.

L

Lafaye, G. "Villa." In *Dictionnaire des Antiquités, grecques et romaines*, edited by Charles Victor Daremberg et Edmond Saglio, 870-891. Paris: Hachette, 1877-1919.

Le Bohec, Yann. *The Imperial Roman Army*. London: Routledge, 2000.

Leleković, Tino and Rendić-Miočević Ante. "Rural Settlements." In *The Archaeology of Roman Southern Pannonia*, edited by Branka Migotti, 270-311. Oxford: BAR International Series 2393, 2012.

Lewit, Tamara. *Villas, Farms and the Late Roman Rural Economy (third to fifth centuries AD)*, BAR Inter. Series 568. Oxford: BAR International Series 568, 2004.

M

Marković, Jovan. *Geografske oblasti SFRJ*. Beograd: Zavod za udžbenike i nastavna sredstva Srbije, 1970.

Mason, D. J. P. "Prata Legionis in Britain." *Britannia* 19 (1988): 163-189.

Maškin, Nikolaj Aleksandrović. *Istorija starog Rima*. (Preveo s ruskog Miroslav Marković) Beograd: Naučna knjiga 1982.

Medović, Aleksandar. "Gamzigradski ratari – dva koraka napred, jedan korak nazad." *RMV* 50 (2008): 151-173.

Medović, Aleksandar. "Arheoznanje – arheoimanje" u poseti jednom sremačkom vikusu iz I ili II veka." *RMV* 52 (2010): 101-111.

Mihajlović, Tatjana. "Antički lokaliteti u okolini Kraljeva." In *Arheološka nalazišta Kruševca i okoline*, edited by Nikola Tasić and Ema Radulović, 223-237. Kruševac-Beograd: Narodni muzej Kruševac, Balkanološki institut SANU, 2001.

Milošević, Petar. "O trasi puta Sirmium – Fossis i Sirmium – Bononia." *Starinar* XXXIX (1989): 117-123.

Mirković, Miroslava. *Rimski gradovi na Dunavu u Gornjoj Meziji*. Dissertationes, Beograd: Arheološko društvo Jugoslavije, 1968.

Mirković, Miroslava. "Eine frühchristiche Inschrif aus der Umgebung von Krupanj." *Arch. Iug.* IX (1968): 91-95.

Mirković, Miroslava. *Sirmium. Its History from the I Century A.D. to 582 A. D. Sirmium* I, Beograd: Institut of Archaeology, 1971.

Mirković, Miroslava. "Beneficijarna stanica kod Novog Pazara." *ŽA* 21 (1971): 263-271.

Mirković, Miroslava. "Ekonomsko socijalni razvoj u II i III veku." In *Istorija srpskog naroda* I, edited by Sima Ćirković, 77-88. Beograd: Spska književna zadruga, 1981.

Mirković, Miroslava. *Viminacium et Margum. IMS*, vol. II, Beograd: *Centre d'études épigraphiques et numismatiques* de la Faculté de philosophie de l'Université de Beograd, 1986.

Mirković, Miroslava. "Rimsko selo Bube kod Singidunuma." *Starinar* XXXIX (1988): 99-104.

Mirković, Miroslava. "Villas et domaines dans l'Illyricum central IV-VI siècle." *ZRVI* XXXV, (1996): 57-75.

Mirković, Miroslava. *Sirmium, istorija rimskog grada od I do kraja VI veka*. Sremska Mitrovica: Blago Sirmijuma, Filozofski fakultet Beograd, 2006.

Mócsy, András. *Die Bevölkerung von Pannonien bis zu den Markomannenkrieg*. Budapest: Verlag der Ungarischen Akademie der Wissenschaften, 1959.

Mócsy, András. "Das Problem der militärischen Territorien in Donauraum." *Acta antique* XX, (1972): 133-168.

Mócsy, András. *Pannonia and Upper Moesia: a history of the middle Danube provinces of the Roman Empire*. London and Boston: Routledge & Kegan Paul Books, 1974.

N

Nelis-Clement, Jocelyne. *Les Beneficiarii: militarises et administrateurs au services de l'Empire (Ire s. a. C. – VIe s.p. C)*. Bordeaux: Ausonius, 2000.

O

Oltean A. Ioana and Hanson, S. William. "Villa settlements in Roman Transylvania." *Journal of Roman Archaeology* 20, (2007): 113-137.

Opra, Ljerka. *Devet hrastova: zapisi o istoriji srpske meteorologije*, Flogiston. Beograd: Republički hidrometeorološki zavod, Muzej nauke i tehnike SANU, Zavod za udžbenike i nastavna sredstva, 1998.

P

Percival, John. *The Roman villa*. London: Book Club Associates, 1981.

Petković, Sofija. "Rimski Gamzigrad pre carske palate." In *Felix Romuliana – Gamzigrad*, edited by Ivana Popović, 33-42. Beograd: Arehološki institut 2010.

Petković, Sofija. "The Roman Settlement on Gamzigrad prior to the Imperial Palace Felix Romuliana." *Starinar* LXI, (2011): 171-190.

Petrović, Dragoljub. "Ostaci rimske građevine u Poskuricama." *Starinar* XV-XVI (1966): 253-256.

Petrović, J. "Ilirsko rimsko blago iz Šabca." *GZM* LIII, (1941): 11-23.

Petrović, Petar. "Nova Trajanova tabla u Đerdapu." *Starinar* XXI (1972): 31-39.

P. Petrović, Petar. *Niš u antičko doba*, Niš: Gradina, 1976.

Petrović, Petar. *Naissus – Remesiana – Horreum Margi, IMS*, vol. IV, Beograd: Centre d'études épigraphiques et numismatiques de la Faculté de philosophie de l'Université de Beograd, 1979.

Petrović, Petar. "O snabdevanju rimskih trupa na Đerdapskom limesu." *Starinar* XXXI (1981): 53-63.

Petrović, Petar. "Sabirni centar za snabdevanje rimskih trupa u Đerdapu." *Starinar* XXXIII-XXXIV (1984): 285-291.

Petrović, Petar. "Classis Flavia Moesica na Dunavu u Gornjoj Meziji." *Starinar* XL-XLI (1991): 207-216.

Petrović, Petar. *Medijana. Rrezidencija rimskih careva.* Beograd-Niš: SANU, Arheološki institut, Narodni muzej-Niš, 1994.

Petrović, Petar. *Timacum Minus et la valée du Timok, IMS,* vol. III/2, Beograd: Centre d'études épigraphiques et numismatiques de la Faculté de philosophie de l'Université de Beograd, 1995.

Petrović, Petar. "Medijana. Antičko naselje sa vilama." *Starinar* XLVII (1997): 295-300.

Petrović, Petar. "Rimljani na Timoku." In *Arheologija istočne Srbije*, edited by Miroslav Lazić, 115-131. Beograd: Centar za arheolški istraživanja, 1997.

Petrović Petar. "Rimski limes na Dunavu u Donjoj Panoniji." *Fruška Gora u antičko doba. Prilozi za staru istoriju i arheologiju*, edited by Nikola Tasić, 9-32. Novi Sad. Matica Srpska 1995.

Petrović, Petar and Bućić, Javorka. "Rimske ciglarske peći i vila u Bakionici kod Požege." *Užički zbornik* 13 (1984): 5-22.

Petrović, Petar and Bućić, Javorka. "Rimska vila u Višesavi kod Bajine Bašte." *Užički zbornik* 15 (1986): 23-42.

Petrović, Petar and Vasić, Miloje. "The Roman frontier in Upper Moesia: Archaeological investigations in the Iron Gate area – main results." In *Roman Limes on the Middle and Lower Danube*, edited by Petar Petrović, 15-26. Belgrade: Archaeological Institute, 1996.

Petrović, Vladimir. "Ekskursi o rimskim starinama na području Đerdapa u delu Bele de Gonde." *Balcanica* XXXIV, (2004): 71-95.

Petrović, Vladimir. Dardanija u rimskim itinerarima. Gradovi i naselja, Beograd: Balkanološki institut SANU, 2007.

Piletić, Dragoslav. "Velike i Male Livadice, antička osmatračnica i kastel." *Starinar* XXXIII-XXXIV (1984): 187-192.

Pop-Lazić, Petar, Jovanović, Aleksandar and Mrkobrad, Dušan. "Novi arheološki nalazi na južnim obroncima Kosmaja." *Glasnik SAD* 8 (1992): 135-143.

Popović, Dragan. "Rekognosciranje u Sremu." *AP* 8 (1966): 186-189.

Popović, Dragan. "Rekognosciranje u Sremu." *AP* 9 (1967): 172-180.

Popović, Dragan. "Rekognosciranje u Sremu." *AP* 10 (1968): 215-224.

Popović, Dragan. "Rekognosciranje u Sremu." *AP* 12 (1970): 194-201.

Popović, Dragan. "Glavna antička komunikacija u Sremu u svetlu arheoloških istraživnja, *Materijali* XVII, Beograd 1980, 101-107.

Popović, Dragan. "Arheološki spomenici u jugoistočnom Sremu." *Zbornik Muzeja Srema* 1 (1995): 9-25.

Popović, Ivana. *Antičko oruđe od gvožđa u Srbiji*. Beograd: Narodni muzej, 1988.

Popović, Ivana. "Notes topographiques sur la region limitrophe entre la Pannonie Seconde et la Mésie Première." *Roman Limes on the Middle and Lower Danube,* edited by Petar Petrović, 137-142. Belgrade: Arheološki institut, 1996.

Popović, Ivana. "Nalazi iz ekonomskog objekta A (lokalitet 31) u sklopu palatijalnog kompleksa Sirmijuma." *Zbornik NM* 20/1 (2011): 335-372.

Popović, Marko. *Beogradska tvrđava*, Beograd: Javno preduzeće "Beogradska tvrđava", 2006.

Popović, Petar. "Konopište – Roman Architectural Complex (I-II century AD)." *Roman Limes on the Middle and Lower Danube,* edited by Petar Petrović, 101-103. Belgrade: Arheološki institut, 1996.

Popović, Vladislav. "Sirmium u 1962 godini." *AP* 4 (1962): 111-119.

Popović, Vladislav. "Sirmium, Sremska Mitrovica – rimski grad." *AP* 5 (1963): 63-73.

Popović, Vladislav. "Sirmium, Sremska Mitrovica – rimski grad." *AP* 7 (1965): 111-114.

Popović, Vladislav. "Uvod u topografiju Viminacijuma." *Starinar* XVIII (1968): 29-53.

Popović, Vladislav. "Donji Milanovac – Veliki Gradac (Taliata), rimsko i ranovizantijsko utvrđenje." *Starinar* XXXIII-XXXIV (1984): 265-282.

R

Rašković, Dušan and Đokić, Nebojiša. "Rezultati rekognosciranja antičkih nalazišta i komunikacija na području južnog Temnića." *Glasnik SAD 13* (1997): 135-146.

Rašković, Dušan. "Rekognosciranje antičkih lokaliteta i komunikacija na području Mojsinjskih i Poslonskih planina." *Glasnik SAD 14* (1997): 171-195.

Rašković, Dušan and Berić, Nikola. "Rezultati rekognosciranja antičkih i sredjovekovnih nalazišta trsteničke opštine i susednih oblasti." *Glasnik SAD 18* (2002): 137-158.

Rickman, Geoffrey. *Roman Granaries and Store Buildings.* Cambridge: University Press, 1971.

Rickman, Geoffrey. *The Corn Supply of Ancient Rome*, Oxford: Univrsity Press Academic Monograph Series, 1980.

Roth, P. Jonathan. *The Logistics of The Roman Army at War (264B.C.-A.D. 235).* Leiden-Boston-Köln: Brill, 1999.

Ružić Mira. "Kržince – Sveti Trojica, kasnoantička vila." In *Arheološka istraživanja E-75*, edited by Marin Brmbolić, 205-225. Beograd: Republički zavod za zaštitu spomenika kulture 2005.

S

Schlüchter, Christian and Jörin, Ueli. "Alpen ohne Gletscher? Holz und Torffunde als Klimaindikatoren." *Die Alpen* 6, 2004: 34-47.

Simić, Zoran. "Lokalitet Katića njive, selo Sokolova, Lazarevac – rimsko naselje, vila." *AP* 23 (1982): 88-90.

Simić, Zoran. "Lokalitet Batašina, naselje Stepojevac, rimska vila." *AP* 23 (1982): 90-93.

Smith, J. Thomas. *Roman Villas: A Study in Social Structure.* London: Routlege, 1997.

Spasić-Đurić, Dragana. *Viminacijum glavni grad rimske provincije Gornje Mezije*, Požarevac: Narodni muzej, 2002.

Spasić-Đurić, Dragana and Jacanović, Dragan. "Trasa puta Viminacijum-Lederata, rezultati mikrorekognosciranja u 2003-2004 godini." *Viminacium* 15 (2007): 123-165.

Srejović, Dragoslav. "Kasnoantička žitnica u Maskaru." *Balcanica* XIII-XIV (1983): 35-43.

Srejović, Dragoslav. "Rimsko poljsko imanje." In *Gamzigrad, kasnoantički carski dvorac*," edited by Stojan Ćelić, 21-23. Beograd: Galerija SANU, 1983.

Srejović, Dragoslav. "Carski dvorac." In *Gamzigrad, kasnoantički carski dvorac*," edited by Stojan Ćelić, 24-95. Beograd: Galerija SANU, 1983.

Srejović, Dragoslav and Cermanović-Kuzmanović, Aleksandrina. *Rečnik grčke i rimske mitologije*, Beograd: Srpska književna zadruga, 1987.

Š

Šabac u prošlosti I, edited by Filipović, S. Šabac: Istorijski arhiv, 1970.

Šašel, Jaroslav. "Rimski natpisi u Đerdapu." In *Limes u Jugoslaviji* I, Zbornik radova sa simposiuma o limesu 1960 godine, edited by Miodrag Grbić, 156-164. Beograd: Societas Archaeologica Iugoslaviae, 1961.

T

Thomas, B. Edit. *Römische Villen in Pannonien, Beiträge zur Pannonischen Siedlungsgeschichte*, Budapest: Akadémiai Kiadó, 1964.

Thomas, B. Edit. "Villa Settlements." In *The Archaeology of Roman Pannonia*, edited by A. Lengyel, and G.T. B. Radan, 275-321. Budapest: The University Press of Kentucky, Akadémiai Kiadó, 1980.

Thomas, Richard and Stallibrass, Sue. "For starters: producing and supplying food to the army in the Roman north-west provinces." In *Feeding the Roman army. The archaeology of production and supply in NW Europe,* edited by Sue Stallibrass and Richard Thomas, 1-17. Oxford: Oxbow Books, 2008.

Todd, M. "Rural Settlement and Society in Britannia." In *Ländliche Besiedlung und Landwirtschaft in den Rhein-Donau-Provinzen des Römischen Reiches*, Vorträge eines internationalen Kolloquiums vom 16.-21. April 1991 in Passau, edited by Helmut Bender and Hartmut Wolff, 101-121. Passau: Marie L. Leidorf, 1994.

Trbuhović, Vojislav and Vasiljević, Milivoje. "Arheološka nalazišta i spomenici u slivu reke Dobrave." *Starinar* XXVII (1977): 153-166.

V

Vasić, Miloje. "Römische Villen von Typus der Villa rustica aus jugoslawischen Boden." *Arch. Iug.* XI (1970): 45-81.

Vasić, Miloje. "Mačva i Podrinje u rimsko doba." *Glasnik SAD* 2 (1985): 124-141.

Vasić, Miloje. *Horreum Margi*, Beograd: Arheološki institut, 1990.

Vasić, Miloje. "Kasnoantička nalazišta u Čačku i okolini." In *Bogorodica Gradačka u istoriji srpskog naroda*, Naučni skup povodom 800 godina Bogorodice Gradačke i grada Čačka 1992, edited by Milovan Vulović, 9-17. Čačak: Narodni muzej 1993.

Vasiljević, Milivoje. "Rekognosciranje – Podrinje." *AP* 14 (1972): 168-189.

Vasiljević, Milivoje. "Rekognosciranje u Podrinju." *AP* 15 (1973): 133-160.

Vasiljević, Milivoje. "Arheološka rekognosciranja u Podrinju." *AP* 21" (1980): 205-228.

Virlouvet, Catherine. *Tessera frumentaria. Les procédures de la distribution du blé public à Rome à la fin de la République et au début de l'Empire*, Rome: École française, 1995.

Vujević, Pavle. "Geopolitiči i fizičko-geografski prikaz Vojvodine." In *Vojvodina I*, edited by Dušan. J. Popović, 1-28. Novi Sad: Istorijsko društvo 1939.

Vujović, Miroslav. "Prilog proučavanju antičkog zidnog slikarstva i štuko dekoracije na tlu Singidunuma." *Singidunum* 1 (1997): 169-179.

Vujović, Miroslav. "New Contributions on the Late Roman Helmets from Irone Gate." *VVM* 39 (2012): 29-43.

Vulić, Nikola. "Vojvodina u rimsko doba." In *Vojvodina* I, edited by Dušan J. Popović, 61-80. Novi Sad: Istorijsko društvo 1939.

Vulić, Nikola. "Antički spomenici naše zemlje." *Spomenik SAN* LXXI (1931): 4-259.

Vulić, Nikola. "Antički spomenici naše zemlje." *Spomenik SAN* XCVIII (1941-48): 1-335.

Z

Zaninović, Marin. "Neki primjeri smještaja antičkih gospodarskih zgrada u obalsko-otočkom području Dalmacije." *Arheološki radovi i rasprave* IV-V (1967): 357-371.

Zaninović, Marin. "Prata legionis u Kosovu kraj Knina s osvrtom na teritorij Tilurija." *Opuscula Archaeologica* 10 (1985): 63-79.

Zotović, Ljubica. "Boljetin (Smorna), rimski i ranovizantijski logor." *Starinar* XXXIII-XXXIV (1984): 211-225.

Ž

Živić, Maja. *Felix Romvliana: 50 godina odgonetanja*. Zaječar: Narodni muzej, 2003.

www.ingramcontent.com/pod-product-compliance
Lightning Source LLC
Chambersburg PA
CBHW061009030426
42334CB00033B/3426